I0058195

SMALL BRAND AMERICA IV
Special Beer Edition: A Look at 26 Craft Breweries

BY
STEVE AKLEY

Written and Published by:
Steve Akley

Text copyright © 2014 Steve Akley
All Rights Reserved

Cover Design © 2014 Mark Hansen
All Rights Reserved

To the Companies Featured in this Book:

It was great working with each and every one of you on this project. Now, it's time to sit back and enjoy our hard work.

CHEERS!

Small Brand America IV
Special Beer Edition: A Look at 26 Craft Breweries

Preface

The first two books in the **Small Brand America** series each took a look at 26 companies and chronicled the struggles of those companies competing on grocer's shelves against megabrands. The third book in the series was a special edition focusing only on companies based in Hawai'i. Readers got a unique perspective of the challenges facing companies so far from the continental United States.

The fourth offering of **Small Brand America** is also a special edition. This book is all about beer. All twenty-six of the companies profiled are craft brewers. They range from small local brands to regional offerings to some which are available on a nationwide basis. Even the largest of the companies featured here, though, pales in comparison when stacking them up against the big players in the industry.

These companies have an additional challenge that goes beyond what most of the companies featured in Small Brand America, which are outside of the world of brewing, have faced, and that's advertising. Make that "mega-advertising." When you think about beer, you almost always associate it with advertising. The commercials used to sell beer transcend product promotion and often become part of popular culture.

An additional challenge craft brewers face is the sheer number of competitors. Whether it's the fact beer is made from simple ingredients, the fun quotient of being involved in an industry where you are equally as enthused about being a consumer or the upside potential for high profits, the beer industry has a lot of competitors. According to the Brewer's Association (*brewersassociation.org*), an organization serving the craft brewing industry, in 2013 the numbers of breweries in the United States surpassed the 2,500 mark.

Despite the stiff competition, like bubbles in a pint glass, the best companies rise up. ***Small Brand America IV*** introduces you to 26 exciting and growing companies from the world of craft brewing. You get fun insight into how the company started, their products, what their organization is like and who is the person behind the brand.

You walk away with a greater appreciation for not only the products, but also what it took to get them on the market. If you ever happen to see one of the beers featured in this book on the shelves of your favorite store, I suggest you pick some up and raise a glass in honor of the company that created it.

After all, each one represents ***Small Brand America***!

Table of Contents

Chapter 26

Chapter 1
Belching Beaver Brewery

980 Park Center Drive, Suite A
Vista, CA 92081
(760) 599-5832

belchingbeaver.com
info@belchingbeaver.com

Established
2012

Leadership
Tom Vogel, Owner & General Manager
Dave Mobley, Owner & Tasting Room Manager
Troy Smith, Master Brewer

"Beer has always been the common man's brew and we want to stick with that."
        -Tom Vogel

Mortgage services and real estate.

That was the world Tom Vogel lived in. You might not think it's a natural path into craft brewing, but Tom sees it differently. He always knew he wanted to open a brewery. It seemed the questions of "when" and "how" were the only two things holding him back.

His first experience with craft beer came at a happy hour in 1996. He tried a Redhook and loved it. The superior quality of this much smaller brand over the large, well-advertised, megabrands was a game changer for him.

While owning his own mortgage/real estate companies, he began making both beer and wine at home. He was so committed to his hobbies he would even plant his own grape vines and take classes to hone his craft. It was at one of these classes where he met Dave Mobley, an architect and fellow at-home wine maker. They began pooling their resources to collaborate on their wine making hobby.

The fun of making beer and wine at home really began to light a spark for Tom to create his own brewery. The ups-and-downs and grind of his job seemed to take the wind out of him when you compared it to the fun of making a living in the world of craft brewing.

The plan really began to take shape at his regular poker game. One of the players, Troy Smith was a brewer at a well-known craft brewery. When Tom spoke to him about his idea of opening his own brewery, he asked Troy what he thought. Troy thought it was a great idea and was willing to leave the company he worked for and work with Tom for an ownership stake in the company. They quickly began working out the details of their planned new brewery.

When Tom's old wine making buddy Dave Mobley heard about the partnership Tom and Troy were working on, he wanted in, too. He conveyed his interest, but Tom politely turned down his request to join them. Tom believed adding a partner who was simply contributing capital (after all, Dave did have a successful career as an architect) wasn't something they needed at the time.

The meeting when Tom turned down Dave's request to join them had been cordial. Even though they wouldn't be business partners, Tom and Dave would remain friends. In fact, they decided to go out for a few drinks afterwards. Soon they were hopping from craft brewer to craft brewer and weighing in on how they could improve each of the breweries.

At the end of the night, Dave turned to Tom and said, "Come on, let's do this." Tom knew he was right, so he welcomed Dave to his proposed new business.

Even though he had initially balked at adding Dave to the mix, it turned out to be a blessing in disguise. Dave's expertise in architecture and building would prove invaluable in starting their business. Tom was able to focus on the paperwork and regulations needed to start a brewery while Dave worked on the location and, ultimately, the build-out when they secured the site for their business.

The name Belching Beaver came at a cocktail party. Tom and his wife were talking about the new craft brewery he was working on with another couple. The woman, whom Tom would later hire for the brewery, came up with the name Belching Beaver. The idea: the hardworking, blue collar beaver, belching from the libations he enjoyed in his spare time, got them laughing… uncontrollably. Soon the ideas of merchandising and the names for the beers they would offer were rolling from these giggling party goers. It was certainly a fun name, and Tom believed it would resonate with how they wanted to represent themselves and their company.

By the end of the cocktail party, it was official; their new company would be called Belching Beaver.

Tom didn't even think twice about the name as he went through the lawyers and legal process to make Belching Beaver the name of his company. Just as he was finishing the arduous process of the legal hurdles to securing the name, his daughter came back from college with some news that shocked Tom.

In what had to be the strangest father/daughter talk of 2012, Tom's daughter informed him her friends told her Belching Beaver was slang for something which didn't equate to a small rodent drinking beer. (Note: The **Small Brand America** team will not be defining the slang version of the name so you will have to refine your search engine skills if you are not familiar with it yourself).

He thought about changing it, but it would have been an expensive and time-consuming proposition. Since they were already moving forward on their brewery, they simply couldn't afford the expense of delaying their launch, so the name Belching Beaver stuck.

Lucky for the team of Tom, Troy and Dave, it did. The name Belching Beaver has accomplished exactly what Tom had envisioned the first time he heard it: laughter. For his loyal customers, the name conveys the light-hearted approach the Belching Beaver team uses with their business. Every person hired for the company has to be fun. Seriously, it's a company rule. You have to be willing to laugh and enjoy a good time.

This focus on not taking yourself too seriously is something the Belching Beaver's customers seem to enjoy as well. The experience of visiting the brewery is guaranteed to be as full of laughs as it is great beer. It's a combination which seems to ensure loyal customers coming back to the Belching Beaver time after time.

It's not to say the name hasn't presented challenges. There are accounts which have been coached by competitors to say the name is offensive and to leave them out. The team has also felt some pushback from the craft brewing industry, as well. Even though there is an inherent renegade spirit to craft brewing, some of the individuals have so focused on the art of brewing, they look down on Belching Beaver for what they think is a lowbrow attempt of distinguishing themselves.

Even though there are times when the name has been a hindrance, Tom remains glad things have worked out as it did. He believes the seriousness of some of his competitors takes on the snobiness often associated with wine production and its customers. He left the serious side when he got out of the mortgage/real estate business. He's sticking to the fun approach.

The great news is not only is it working, it's working really well. Belching Beaver is growing at a stratospheric rate. With their current capacity of 7,200 barrels, they are brewing 24 hours a day. They are increasing capacity soon to 12,000 barrels but are forecasting to outgrow their capacity again within six months.

As such, they are currently searching for a new facility where they can increase production to 20,000 barrels. Then the plan is to simply catch their breath. At least for a moment.

How are they growing so quickly?

Well, if you are a fan of the CBS TV show Survivor, you often hear Jeff Probst deliver the line, "The tribe has spoken." It seems the general population isn't offended by a belching beaver; they love it. The company recently added two sales reps and grew from a handful of direct accounts to over four hundred in less than four months.

Wouldn't you have loved to have been a fly on the wall when Tom's daughter was explaining to him what her college friends told her they thought a belching beaver meant?

Belching Beaver Brewery Photo Album

Mike (Assistant Brewer), Dave Mobley, Jenny Vogel (Tom's wife), Tom Vogel, Diane (Came up with the name Belching Beaver), Troy Smith (Head Brewer)

Friday night event at the brewery

The Belching Beaver team

Community event

Merchandise

Production

Serving beer and smiles

Peanut Butter Flavored Milk Stout? #megaawesome

Belching Beaver product lineup

Chapter 2
Blue Pants Brewery

500 Lanier Road, Bldg. 1
Madison, AL 35758

bluepantsbrew.com
pants@bluepantsbrew.com

Established
2010

Leadership
Michael Spratley, Owner

"We have a target in mind where we will say, 'Yes, that's big enough,' and we look forward to making that statement."
    -Michael Spratley

It seems like the days of beer simply being hops, grains, yeast and water are gone. Exciting new ingredients and brewing techniques have brought more flavor profiles and excitement to beer than anyone could have ever imagined just a few short years ago. You could almost make the statement craft brewing has turned the beer industry into rocket science.

Taking this into consideration, perhaps it's no coincidence Blue Pants Brewery is helmed by aerospace engineer Michael Spratley. Maybe Michael's education and background is the secret weapon in the company's rapid ascent in the craft brewing world. (Bring a rocket scientist and their intellectual approach to brewing beer and growing the brand.)

Michael's career didn't start out with dreams of owning and operating a craft brewery. He was from Madison, Alabama, not far from the U.S. Space and Rocket Center in Huntsville, Alabama. Seemingly, specializing in aerospace engineering was the perfect educational fit for someone in an area with an abundance of opportunities in the field.

Michael got his undergraduate degree from the University of Michigan, but it was only the second most important event which occurred during his time in the state. It was there he also met Allison, his future wife.

After graduation, the two moved to Seattle, Washington, for an internship Michael secured at Boeing. The knowledge and experience he picked up during his internship would prove to be only the second most impactful thing that occurred in his life there. (Notice a theme?)

While in Washington, Michael also got into the rich craft brewing scene. He found the products available at the plentiful local brewpubs and craft breweries to far exceed the quality of the selection of beers he was used to getting back home in Alabama. In fact, Alabama's laws tended to be pretty tight on the beer industry in general at the time. It was not uncommon to have residents from Madison, who enjoyed craft beer, to make a run to nearby Tennessee to pick up some of the unique beers which were just starting to pick up steam in the early 2000s.

After completing his internship in Seattle, Michael and Allison moved to Georgia where Michael got his graduate degree at the Georgia Institute of Technology. Of course, going from the beer landscape in Seattle to Atlanta where the Georgia Institute of Technology resided was a letdown in terms of being able to find an abundance of craft breweries. Still, Atlanta was a big place, and there was some degree of a craft brew scene, even if it paled in comparison to Seattle.

After completing his schooling in Georgia, Michael and Allison moved back to Michael's home of Madison, Alabama. Madison, on the other hand, hadn't really embraced the craft beer revolution, just yet. As such, Michael began homebrewing to see if he could create some unique flavor profiles like he had experienced back in Seattle (this was despite the fact it was illegal at the time to homebrew in Alabama… again, they hadn't yet embraced craft brewing and brewing beer at home wouldn't actually become legal in Alabama until 2013).

Soon, Michael was getting rave reviews from friends, family members, neighbors and co-workers. He even started to take a few of his beers to local bars to ask the proprietors if it was available commercially, would it be a product they would be willing to carry in their establishment. The feedback was positive so Michael began to seriously think about starting his own brewery.

At the time, he was working for the military, specializing in the drone program. He was involved in testing (how well they fly, safety issues, etc.) and the purchasing of drones. He had a solid career in an industry in which he had spent years training to work. Still, the thought of making something through his own sweat and creativity for others to enjoy appealed to him even more than working in aerospace.

Rather than simply opening a business, Michael decided to take a tactical approach to starting a craft brewery. His idea was to find a small space with low rent where he could brew in his spare time. From there, he could slowly work his way into starting a bigger operation without simply quitting his job and jumping in.

He secured a 400 square foot commercial area which only cost him about $200 per month to rent. Rather than buy the expensive equipment which goes into opening a brewery, he designed and built a system himself utilizing steel barrels he got for free (we are talking about an engineer here, folks).

Under the name Blue Pants Brewery, he began making beer out of his mini-craft brewery. The name came from the combination of the nicknames he and his wife have. Pants was Michael's nickname from college (don't even ask, he's not going to tell you that story) and "blue" came from the nickname Michael gave his wife Allison based on the color of her eyes (they are hazel... just kidding, they are blue, of course).

The brewery Michael started was a family affair with everyone working in their spare time to help out. Michael would brew on the weekends and clean in the evenings during the week. His brother Clint would help with sales and his other brother Albert assisted with IT. Michael's parents helped out with a little bit of everything when needed.

Michael notes that starting out with a brewery in 400 square feet is a great way to test the interest of the market in your product. It's also a great way to get a personal feel for your ability to transition out of your job and into craft brewing full-time. One thing it is not, though, is a great way to make outstanding beer. Michael acknowledges the space and equipment limitations meant he wasn't putting out the best quality of product he could. Plus, he had no opportunity to scale the business up where he was located. If he wanted to pursue this as a real business, at some point he was going to finally have to take a leap of faith and simply say, "I'm doing this."

After about eight months of saying, "We need to do this," he finally committed to going to a larger space and buying a 15 barrel system. Still, he didn't quite go all the way by quitting his job. For the next year-and-a-half, he continued to work his job and utilized his vacation and sick time to supplement extra hours at the brewery when needed.

Finally, in August of 2012, he was at the point where having two careers wasn't possible. He left his job and became the first full-time employee at Blue Pants (again, don't even think about getting the "pants" part of the story).

Derek Weidenthal, another home brewing enthusiast, would quickly become the brewery's second employee. Michael sent Derek to the Seibel Institute in Chicago to secure his professional degree as a brewmaster. This freed up Michael to turn over the bulk of the brewing duties to him so he could manage the company and work on growing sales.

Through the hard work of a lobbyist group called Free the Hops, over time, Alabama's laws surrounding beer production, sale and consumption, have been favorably changed. For instance, when Blue Pants started, they weren't allowed to a have a taproom where patrons could sample beers and buy it by the glass. These tend to be the lifeblood of craft brewers because they create revenue streams and give potential customers the opportunity to try beers which tend to be quite different from what they are typically used to buying.

Currently, the group is working on amending the law to allow craft brewers to sell packaged beer to go. This would be the final component to really allow Blue Pants to complete the customer experience of visiting, touring, tasting and walking away with their favorite beer selection.

The company has evolved in many ways from their time in the 400 square foot facility, as well. Their beer no longer suffers from the quality issues they experienced early on. Brewmaster Derek Weidenthal continues to innovate with their beer offerings. In fact, four of the ten taps in Blue Pants' taproom are dedicated to experimental beers.

Their labeling has also vastly improved over time. The unique stick figure drawings of Michael's high school friend Charles Acker gives the company a unique and fun feel. Something you would totally expect from a company named Blue Pants!

Currently, Blue Pants can be found in Alabama, Tennessee and Mississippi. There are plans to continue to grow and expand the brand until they get to the sweet spot where they are as large as they are comfortable being. Michael wants to lead them to the line of perfection where they are able to balance revenue and quality.

Michael Spratley notes that this is one of the aspects he loves about the business. It's challenging to build a brand in an extremely competitive and constantly changing market. He simply says, "You have to continually learn how to play the game better. That's the way you win, and it's fun trying to figure out exactly how to do that."

Wow, it sounds like the approach of a person who really likes to breakdown what it takes to be successful. Almost like an engineer.

Imagine that!

Don't ask about the pants story, though. He's not telling that one!

Blue Pants Brewery Photo Album

Allison (Blue) & Michael (Pants) Spratley

The entire Spratley family has helped out with the company at times (pictured here at the build-out of the company's original brewery)

Michael's homemade barrels he used at his original brewery

Inside of the new Blue Pants Brewery

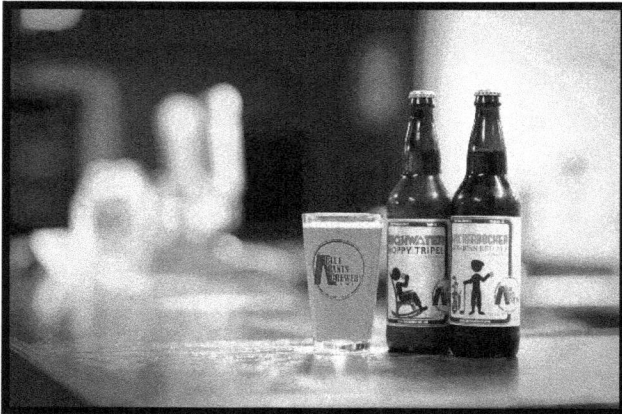

Blue Pants Brewery product lineup

Chapter 3
Brooklyn Brewery

79 North 11th Street
Brooklyn, NY 11249
(718) 486-7422

brooklynbrewery.com
info@brooklynbrewery.com

Established
1988

Leadership
Steve Hindy, Co-Founder and President

"I was in the audience behind Egyptian President Anwar Sadat when he was assassinated in 1981."
        -Steve Hindy

In 1981, the world didn't have the media proliferation like we have today. We didn't have multiple 24 hour news channels giving us access to a constant stream of what was going on in the world. Nor did we have the internet, so there were no bloggers or people "tweeting" live as events occurred.

Depending on how you personally interpret that statement, you may consider it the stone age of media (a general lack of knowledge reported via a comparative few entities) or the golden age of media (a time when professional reporters reported real news not doing a 15 minute segment on what Kim Kardashian wore to the grocery store that day).

In 1981, as the Associated Press (A.P.) correspondent who happened to be on the scene at the time when Egyptian President Anwar Sadat was assassinated, Steve Hindy would literally be at the center of the world. With the eyes of the entire world figuratively on him, it was his job to report what was going on in this chaotic scene. Anyone else would likely spend the rest of their career in the media feasting off of that one event, trying to see if they could once again land that one big story. Steve Hindy is different, though. For him, his reporting career perhaps became the most unique footnote in craft brewing history, but it truly ended up being the second most important job he ever did.

The biggest thing Steve Hindy has ever done wasn't reporting to the world the assassination of Anwar Sadat. It was the starting of Brooklyn Brewery in 1988. He started his business at the beginning of the craft beer revolution, and he has managed to keep his company at the forefront of this rapidly emerging and changing industry.

Believe it or not, it all started with his reporting…

Right out of college Steve began working at a small weekly newspaper in upstate New York. He was only there a few weeks before moving on to a larger paper. This scenario repeated a few more times before he got his big break, a job working for A.P. in Newark. With an interest in issues of the time, Steve requested an assignment in Beirut to cover the Lebanese Civil War, which was going on at the time. He was told it wasn't something people normally asked to do, but he persisted and even began studying Arabic.

Finally, after a year of requesting to go, in 1979, Steve Hindy was sent over as the A.P.'s Middle East correspondent. He would spend five years there covering events, such as the Iran hostage crisis, the Iran/Iraq war, the Israeli invasion of 1982 and the aforementioned assassination of Anwar Sadat.

As you can imagine, the job was dangerous. You may envision Steve with a notebook in his hand, a camera around his neck and two guards with machine guns flanking him as he gets in the center of these very dangerous situations where laws, societal rules and social decorum are simply cast aside. Well, the notebook and the camera might be accurate, but there were no armed guards. As a foreign correspondent, Steve was on his own to report the news and do his best to avoid becoming the story. He wasn't always successful doing that. In 1980, he, along with some colleagues, were abducted by a militia group. Two members of their party were tortured and killed and a third was shot multiple times. Steve helped carry him to the helicopter when they were released (luckily, the man did survive his wounds).

You may now be asking, "How can his time in the Middle East lead Steve Hindy to owning the Brooklyn Brewery?"

The whole time Steve was covering the Middle East he was living around and interacting with American diplomats. It seemed all of them enjoyed homebrewing as a hobby since they weren't able to buy beer in the Muslim countries they were living in. Still, this passion for making his own beer probably wouldn't have evolved into the Brooklyn Brewery had it not been for Steve's wife Ellen.

In 1984, when the Philippines began experiencing the unrest which ultimately would lead to the ousting of then President Ferdinand Marcos, the A.P. assigned Steve to go there. Ellen had enough of life as the wife of a war correspondent. She told Steve he could go to the Philippines if he liked, but she was taking the kids and heading back to New York. Living in the Philippines without his family wasn't going to work for Steve. Ellen's conversation had been eye-opening, as well. Steve was a father and husband above anything else, so he took a job at **Newsday** and moved back to New York.

As respected of a publication as **Newsday** was, it just didn't fulfill him like his reporting in the Middle East for the A.P. had. As he was continuing his homebrewing hobby back in the U.S., he began to think about developing a business plan to open a brewery. When a neighbor, Tom Potter, committed to joining him in this new endeavor, they began to get serious about following through on the plan.

Getting the company name and branding proved to be an early challenge. Steve and Tom interviewed more than 30 design firms to try to get the feel for what they wanted to take to market. Of course, they were a start-up, so they were trying to get this done on the cheap, and the quality of the work being submitted reflected it. Once again, Ellen was the voice of reason one day when she saw the frustration of trying all of the various potential vendors. She reminded

Steve New York is home to the best ad agencies in the world. He simply needed to contact them.

Steve decided to heed Ellen's advice and go right to the top. He contacted legendary ad man Milton Glaser. Those in the know will tell you Milton is one of the inspirations for the TV show *Mad Men* (he has done some work for the show, by the way). Of course you don't simply pick up the phone and talk to Milton Glaser… especially when you are a start-up firm. Steve Hindy tried to do exactly that and, as expected, was stopped by the gatekeeper. Despite the rebuff, he continued to try to reach Mr. Glaser, calling every day and speaking to the same woman. Finally, they started to develop a friendly relationship, and one day Milton Glaser happened to be by her desk when Steve called, and she handed the phone to Milton!

With no prep work, Milton, the creative genius he is, was able to instantly help Steve and was gracious in answering his questions. He even resolved the issue of the name in their first call. Steve had been toying with the idea of calling the company Brooklyn Eagle Beer as a tribute to the legendary newspaper once edited by Walt Whitman. Milton instructed him to go with the cleaner Brooklyn Brewery, and the name was born.

The relationship between Steve and Milton continues to this day. Milton, an octogenarian, continues to work, and Steve attributes much of the company's success to Milton's branding initiatives, most important of which was the company name from that first phone call. Having Brooklyn in the name is a calling card which opens doors for them today and has really been key in their international expansions.

With the name and branding secured, Steve and Tom were ready to move forward. Just as they were ready to go, fellow Brooklyn resident Sophia Collier had a frank talk with them.

Sophia had launched Soho Natural Soda on her own a decade before. Going through the normal distribution channels, she couldn't get her soda onto store shelves. The megabrands dominated the shelf space and the channels to get to market. When she finally started self-distributing by calling on the stores herself, she quickly began to gain traction. In the end, she was able to sell her company to Seagram Beverage Company for 15 million dollars.

The conversation with Sophia changed everything for Steve and Tom. They knew they couldn't afford to fully invest in a brewery as well as the trucks and resources required to be in the distribution business. Sophia had been so compelling in her explanation, they knew they needed to follow her lead and go the self-distribution route so they elected to outsource the brewing of their beer (under their formula and direction), and they would distribute the product. The plan worked perfectly. Steve and Tom didn't have the capital investment in a brewery, and with their focus on distribution, they were able to create the channels to get their product into the hands of consumers. As craft distilling began to increase in popularity, the company added other breweries' beers to the mix, as well.

The revenue generated from their successful distribution company led them to finally opening up their own brewery in Brooklyn in 1996. Then New York Mayor Rudy Giuliani was on-hand to cut the ribbon and serve up drinks to the press covering the new business opening. He joked with the reporters covering the event about Steve's transition from a reporter to a brewery owner by stating, "Steve Hindy used to be a journalist but now he is making an honest living."

You wouldn't know it at the time, but Brooklyn Brewery was at the beginning of a revival to the neighborhood they now resided in. A typical Friday night would generate about a dozen people when they first opened. Today, it's not uncommon for 3,000 – 4,000 people to visit on a weekend. Brooklyn Brewery literally had one account in the neighborhood selling their beer when they opened; now they have over 300.

Even the name Brooklyn has become trendy. They were the only consumer packaged goods company with Brooklyn in its name when they started in 1988. There are now over 100. Brooklyn Brewery sold their distribution company in 2003 for twelve million dollars!

The company has rapidly expanded to full capacity in their current location. They are currently looking at opening a second brewery and a third outside of Brooklyn to handle the growing demand domestically and internationally for their beer.

Garrett Oliver, the company's brewmaster, is as well-known and respected as the company itself. He is a frequent guest on TV shows as an industry expert and has written a book entitled **The Brewmaster's Table** about food and beer and serves as the editor-in-chief of the prestigious **Oxford Companion to Beer**. Steve Hindy has also continued his writing. He wrote a book entitled, **Beer School** about the ups-and-downs of starting the Brooklyn Brewery and **The Craft Beer Revolution** about the craft beer industry. He also has plans for a third book featuring the stories of his time covering the Middle East.

With all of his life experiences, the work he is doing now with the Brooklyn Brewery is the most rewarding. Now that is saying something. Let's not forget, this is a man who witnessed the assassination of Anwar Sadat, served as a war reporter in multiple conflicts, was captured himself by radical militants and even witnessed a rousing speech by Ayatollah Khomeini in Khomeini's hometown!

Brooklyn Brewery Photo Album

Steve Hindy

Steve Hindy in his A.P. days meeting Egyptian President Hosni Mubarak

Brewmaster Garrett Oliver

The entrance to Brooklyn Brewery

A tour of the facility

Brooklyn Brewery product lineup

Chapter 4
Cape Cod Beer

1336 Phinneys Lane
Hyannis, MA 02601
(508) 790-4200

capecodbeer.com
info@capecodbeer.com

Established
2004

Leadership
Todd Marcus, Brewmaster and President
Beth Marcus, Business Manager

"We want to be Cape Cod's beer."
        -Beth Marcus

Prior to owning their own brewery, Boston residents Todd and Beth Marcus were working stiffs in corporate jobs like the rest of us. Todd was an electrical engineer in the biotech industry. Beth worked in the software industry as a consultant. One of the many passions the couple shared was a love for good beer. Not only was Todd a hobbyist homebrewer, many of their travels were tied to visiting breweries, trying different beers and buying t-shirts and gear from their favorite stops.

Even though it's difficult at the time, often our most challenging moments give birth to our greatest accomplishments. While there isn't a direct tie to Todd and Beth's lowest moment leading directly to them owning their own brewery, there certainly is a dotted line.

The low point came when Todd lost his job. The firm he worked for was scaling back, and they laid off all of the engineers. Todd was out of work and trying to decide what to do. You are probably thinking, "Just start a brewery," but the notion of opening a craft beer company wasn't anything being seriously considered at that point.

He ended up securing a job in the gaming industry where he was responsible for the design and building of some of the company's devices. Just when he thought he was past the lowest point by getting back to the job pool, he realized misery in a job can be just as bad as having no job. Todd quickly surmised what he was doing was more along the lines of assembly rather than his area of expertise in engineering.

Knowing he was an avid homebrewer, a friend who had a business selling stainless steel taps to the brewing industry, invited him to a brewer's dinner. The timing was perfect. He was stressed out about his job and was looking for a fun night out. You have to understand that this was the late 90s, long before these sort of events were commonplace like they are now.

At the dinner, Todd was immediately swept up into the electric feel of the excitement from the attendees. There were brewers from across the country sharing stories about some of the great things they were doing with the beers they were making.

While still there, Todd phoned home to Beth and said, "I know what I want to do with my life. I want to open a brewery."

Beth retorted, "Stop it. You are drunk."

Todd came right back with, "Maybe, but I do want to be in this business."

Even as the beer wore off, Todd's enthusiasm did not. He immediately began searching for a job in the industry. He ended up finding a brewery in Vermont hiring. He spoke with the owner who also happened to be an engineer. Even without industry experience, the engineer bond was enough to land him the job.

Todd and Beth were young and didn't have children yet, so they were ready for an adventure. With Beth commuting every week to Boston to work, they lived in Vermont, and Todd started learning the business-side of making beer.

He worked there about six months before moving to another brewer in Maine (Beth still continued to commute back to Boston every week). After another six months there, Todd landed a job with a company which operated brewpubs.

They were opening a new restaurant/brewery in Pennsylvania, just outside of Philadelphia.

They did settle in Pennsylvania for a while, even having their first child while living there. They often found themselves driving back to Boston, though, to be near their family. Growing tired of commute back and forth, Todd started looking for a job at a brewery in Boston.

When he came up empty on the job search, he started fanning outwards from Boston. He found an opportunity at a brewpub in Hyannis, Massachusetts. While this didn't get them back to Boston, it did get them back to the state and much closer to family. In January of 1999, Todd took the job, and he and Beth bought a house in Hyannis.

Initially, it was going well. The restaurant and the brewery both were doing great. Things began to change when the owners decided to sell out. New owners came in, but they struggled with running the business, and they also sold out.

A few changes of ownership in such short order in the restaurant business tends to damage a reputation in the market. Unfortunately, they were no exception. The company really began to struggle. Two weeks before Christmas of 2003, the owners informed Todd they wouldn't be able to pay him any longer. When things go bad, they really seem to go bad, so, of course, Beth also lost her job about two weeks after Christmas.

Okay, maybe that part about being at their "low point" earlier in the chapter may have been a bit premature. The Marcus family, now with two children, started 2004 with no income.

Just like the earlier challenges when Todd lost his job and then found himself with a job he didn't want, the personal horror they were living actually led to new opportunities for the Marcuses.

Their idea was a unique one. The restaurant side of the brewpub where Todd had worked was still in operation. The plan he and Beth came up with was they would finally open up their own brewery. Todd would utilize the equipment in the 500 square foot brewery in exchange for brewing the beer to supply the restaurant customers.

The desperate owners took them up on their offer, and Cape Cod Beer was born. Todd and Beth chose the name based on how easy it rolled from the tongue. They wanted to make it easy for a customer to order their beer. Something like Cape Cod Brewing Company seemed too formal and clunky. The simplicity of Cape Cod Beer just worked.

Their first beer was delivered in mid-April of 2004. Soon, Todd would acquire 12 customers in the area. He would brew the beer, package it in kegs and deliver it to his customers out of the back of Beth's minivan.

While everything seemed to be going great with the brewery, those old problems with the restaurant began to pop up again. Soon, the restaurant was in bankruptcy, though Cape Cod Beer was able to continue to run its business out of the restaurant as a separate entity.

In 2006, they finally moved to their own facility which at 3,000 square feet seemed like an unfathomable amount of space compared to their old set-up. Even with the increased capacity, Todd and Beth made a key strategic decision designed to ensure a quality product for their customers while maintaining profitability for them. They elected to self-distribute their product. This afforded them a plethora of advantages in addition to keeping more revenue in the company. First, they can ensure their product remains refrigerated from production, through distribution and in the store. This keeps their beer as fresh as possible.

Secondly, self-distributing also means they can maintain direct relationships with the stores which sell their products. Using a distributor would have meant their product would have left Cape Cod and then be brought back in. Distributors like to gain efficiency by visiting the stores less so they tend to overload them leading to out-of-date products on the shelves. Cape Cod can actually sell just what they need. If the store gets a run on their beer, with a delivery area of just 50 miles for them to cover the entire Cape, they can bring product in right away. It's this sort of customer service which makes retailers want to sell their product.

Another strategic initiative Todd and Beth adhere to is they try to keep their business spend local whenever possible. Whether it's raw ingredients, the use of a vendor or even the gifts and gear they sell in their store, they try to buy local. Beth proudly notes that looking at the dollars spent on their gift store items, 75% of every dollar spent goes right back into Cape Cod.

One of the cool areas where their dollars are kept local is on their tap handles. They used to buy them from an internet retailer. Of course, this just ends up with a reworked version of the tap handles everyone else has.

After purchasing a metal sculpture which hangs over their fireplace from local artist Steve Swain, Todd and Beth were able to convince him to create some tap handles for them. This has not only invested dollars back into the local economy, it has given Cape Cod Beer a unique identity in local bars since the company's tap handles are truly each a unique work of art.

A visit to their facility is a pretty unique experience, as well. You see the raw ingredients, learn about the process and even sample some of the beers. They have a biergarten which actually moves indoors for the long Cape Cod winters! There is also something else pretty unique right outside of the brewery. In 2013, Todd and Beth's older son Jacob (then 14) was looking for a job. Being only 14, he found securing employment to be a challenge. When Todd found a hotdog truck on Craigslist, he convinced Beth it would be a great way to teach their sons about running a business.

The first summer, Beth spent a lot of time helping manage the hot dog truck. In 2014, Jacob was on his own. He's had the usual challenges of running a business. Securing raw ingredients, profitability and dealing with part-time workers… compounded by the fact these are often his friends and schoolmates. Overall, it's been a great experience for him, and it's a great pairing with their business.

Cape Cod Beer recently turned 10 years old. For Todd and Beth they are right on track where they want to be. Their product is beloved by the locals and craved by the visitors. They are at a time where they could look to simply sustaining what they have and organically growing their business in Cape Cod or trying to expand their reach further. With a recent expansion to their brewery, they are simply taking a moment to catch their breath.

Hey, who can blame them?

They've been walking uphill for quite a while after cratering out a few times over the years. They have a great thing going with Cape Cod Beer and they simply want to enjoy their beer, their family, their employees and their customers.

Actually, that sounds like a pretty good plan!

Cape Cod Beer Photo Album

Todd and Beth Marcus

The brewery (outside)

The brewery (inside)

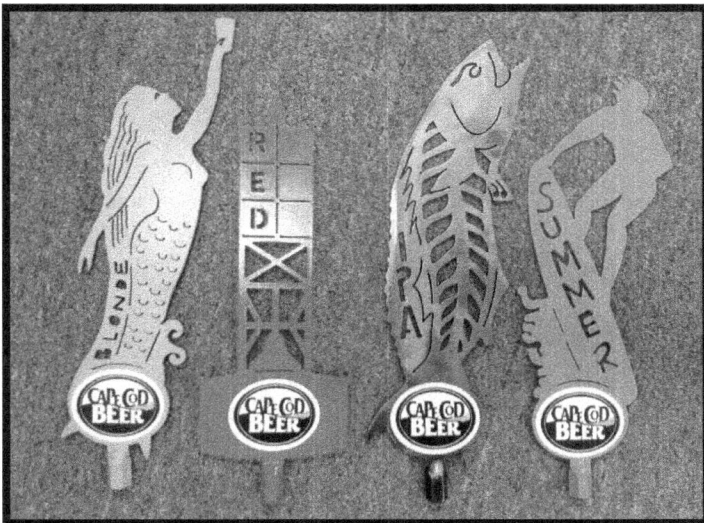

Some of Cape Cod Beer's famous tap handles

Going for a swim

Cape Cod Beer product lineup

Chapter 5
Dale Bros. Brewery

2120 Porterfield Way
Upland, CA 91786
(909) 579-0032

dalesbrosbrewery.com
blacksheep@dalebrosbrewery.com

Established
2003

Leadership
Curt Dale, Founder and Co-Owner
Andy Dale, Co-Owner

"It took me almost a year and a half to secure a location, get the appropriate licensing, build out a brewery and get together a recipe I was ready to bring to market."
  -Curt Dale

A biography of brothers Curt and Andy Dale could easily be a montage of scenery of the United States set to the famous Johnny Cash tune, *"I've Been Everywhere."* After all, at one point or another, one, or both of the brothers called all of the following home: Upland, California (truly home as it is where they were born, started their business and reside now), Claremont, California, Manchester, Vermont, Chicago, Illinois, Denver, Colorado, Louisville, Kentucky and Boston, Massachusetts. Heck, if they would have tossed in Baraboo and Waterloo the song would have been complete!

Despite an age difference of six years, and separation of up to thousands of miles between the two, beer always served as a bond for the brothers. Ultimately, it would also be beer which would bring the two back together and have them working side-by-side building up their namesake business.

Curt, the elder of the two brothers, became interested in homebrewing after trying Guinness Stout. It was his first exposure to a beer other than the typical German pilsners most of the large nationwide companies offered. The concept of individuals making beer at their houses was just getting its start back then as Jimmy Carter had signed a law allowing individuals to homebrew for personal consumption only a few years before.

From 1980 – 1987, he was a pretty avid homebrewer, and over time, he really refined his craft with each offering seemingly better than the previous. When he went to work for an urban planning software firm, he found he had less time to brew himself and ended up giving up his hobby.

Meanwhile, younger brother Andy picked up homebrewing as a hobby not long after Curt had stopped brewing. His interest in craft brewing rekindled Curt's love for making beer, and soon he was also back involved in the hobby with his brother.

Though their beer was just for friends, family members and themselves, the guys took their craft seriously enough to go as far as to labeling their beer. Since it was a collaborative effort, Curt designed labels with the name Dale Bros. Brewery. They even frequently discussed starting their own brewery, and a few times they had started down the path on launching a business, but parameters would change, and they would decide against it.

Cue the Johnny Cash.

After graduation, the hobbyist brewing brothers would once again be separated. Like Curt, Andy ended up working in the tech sector (in editing and special effects), but he took a job in Boston, Massachusetts 3,000 miles away. It looked like Dale Bros. was going to be an East Coast/West Coast operation with each brother brewing on his own.

At the time, 2001, home theaters were just becoming trendy. In particular, out in California where Curt was still living, home owners were interested in adding a media room. One day, the owner of the urban planning software company Curt worked for came into the office and announced he was closing the company and starting a home theater installation company. Everyone who currently worked with him was out of a job.

Yikes!

While the sudden loss of a job is traumatic for most people, Curt knew exactly what he was going to do. This was the jolt he needed to get his craft brewery going. Whether it was a premonition that Andy, who now lived across the continent with a family of his own, would eventually join him or the fact he was trying to capture the magic the two brothers had when they brewed together, Curt went with the name Dale Bros. Brewery, even though he was the only Dale involved in the company at the time.

It took a while (more than a year) but eventually Curt was able to find some used equipment, a small space in a business park and get the state and federal licensing needed to open the business. The federal paperwork had been delayed largely due to the low priority the Bureau of Alcohol, Tobacco and Firearms put on licensing at the time as this was fairly soon after the tragedy of September 11th.

Another challenge was Curt had to figure out exactly how the equipment worked on his own as he had to complete the build-out himself. In all, it took another five months to figure out all the equipment and brew a couple of recipes before he had refined the ingredients for a beer he wanted to sell.

He had utilized the American Brewers Guild to not only learn more about brewing but to show him the fundamentals of running the brewery as well. The challenge came in how to approach it all, mostly because he was wearing so many hats in getting started (brewer, cellarman, bottling, sales, delivery, bookkeeping, accounting, etc.).

From Andy's perspective, even though Curt had conveyed his desire to have Andy join him, especially to help with the sales side of the business (Curt was more into the process and brewing side) he had no intention of joining Curt back in California. Life was going pretty well for him on the East Coast in Boston.

Then one day his company announced a major re-organization of the company. Andy was going to be shifted to a less desirable are of the company. His child was just getting ready to enter kindergarten. His wife was from Arizona so a move to California would put her closer to her family. For him, he had his brother still hoping he would join him in Dale Bros. back in Upland, California.

In 2007, Andy and his wife made the decision to pick up stakes in Boston and move to California. Dale Bros. Brewery was now officially going to be a company run by the Dale brothers (thankfully no false advertisement lawsuits had been filed as a result of the fact there had only been one brother in the company prior to Andy joining).

Early on, the brothers made inroads into their local market by serving as the unofficial on-premise beer company for backyard parties in the area. It was a niche market they serviced and was a very profitable segment for them. They would brew the beer, deliver it and even set up the keg(s) at the party. Word-of-mouth about their beer as the "backyard beer providers" of Upland helped them greatly when they began increasing their focus on packaged distribution (bottles) through distributors.

From 2007 (when Andy joined) until early 2012, the brothers grew their business slowly and organically. In 2012, they took the next step in increasing their business by getting help with the graphics for their company. Before enlisting a professional marketing company, Curt designed the labels and Andy handled collateral material and their website. The company they used kept their general look and design but gave it a much more professional feel.

In 2013, they moved to a new facility which afforded them the luxury of connecting with customers by offering tours and a tap room. Often, they take their connection further by offering up their facility to the community and donating a portion of their beer sales to the charitable causes. They also have some great outdoor space at the site and with the great weather in Upland, their biergarten has become a popular gathering spot.

The brothers realize they are at a very interesting time in what is to become the story of their company. For the first five years they worked together, simple survival was the order of the day, and they never looked very far ahead with their business plans. With their packaging and labeling complete, and their new facility introducing their product to many new customers every day, the brothers realize they need to identify not only who they are, but what they want to be.

Questions like should they look further into self-distributing versus utilizing distributors? Can they do something more with the open space surrounding their building? (They have a great relationship with their landlord.) What is their exit strategy?

These are open issues they look to address in the near future and are issues they want to address sooner rather than later.

If things play out like they always have for Curt and Andy Dale, it's probably a safe guess that another brewery in Baraboo may be opened and a distribution center in Waterloo will be in the mix, as well.

Fade out the Johnny Cash.

Dale Bros. Brewery Photo Album

Andy and Curt Dale

The brew team

Outside the brewery

Inside the brewery

Tasting room crew

Distribution team

Hops harvest

Dale Bros. Brewery product lineup

Chapter 6
Dead Armadillo Craft Brewing

3764 E. 48th Place
Tulsa, OK 74135
(918) 232-8627

dabrewery.com
breweryinfo@dabrewery.com

Established
2013

Leadership
Mason Beercroft, Co-Founder
Tony Peck, Co-Founder

"Before we knew it we went from fun conversations to actually owning our own brewery."
     -Tony Peck

After graduation from Emporia State in Kansas, Tony Peck, an IT programmer and hobby brewer, settled in Tulsa, Oklahoma. There he joined the local Lutheran church. It just so happened the pastor of the church, Mason Beercroft was also a homebrewer. The two immediately bonded over their combined interest in formulating the perfect beer.

Tony had first started brewing in 2006. Over time, he continued to ratchet up his offerings by investing in better ingredients, newer equipment and refining his skills through practice. At the same time, Pastor Beercroft (seems oddly appropriate) was incorporating his love of brewing beer into his work at the church.

He had started brewing when a friend introduced it to him while he was attending the seminary. He moved several times after completing his education prior to his relocation to Tulsa where he would meet Tony. Each step of the way, he would continue to homebrew and incorporate his beer making into church events.

Offering his tasty homebrews made for some pretty unique and fun church outings. Mason would bring his beer to church functions for parishioners to enjoy. He taught classes about homebrewing to members of the congregation and utilized his skills to appeal to those who shared his passion for great beer. A perfect example was the time he had a vacation bible school for the kids while the adults enjoyed his beers outside on the porch. (Mason proudly mentions there was a sizeable increase in parental involvement in vacation bible school when tied to his beer mixers).

When Tony began attending the church where Mason was serving as the pastor, he and Mason would share tips on process and ingredients to help each other refine their offerings. In 2011, Mason was going through a professional change whereby he was leaving the church as a pastor to become a writer for a spiritual magazine (though most of his writings for the publication tend to be along the lines of human interest stories). While he was working a corporate job, Tony always had an entrepreneurial mindset as his parents had owned restaurants back in his childhood hometown of Chanute, Kansas.

Between Tony's interest in looking for an opportunity to start a business, and Mason's flexibility as a writer, the two began to formulate a plan to start their own brewery. At first, it wasn't much more than just talk between two friends who enjoyed brewing beer together.

Over time, these long talks over their shared craft beers did start to shape-up and begin to look like a business, but still it wasn't readily apparent they would act upon these plans. They were seemingly as "pie in the sky" as they were a true working business plan they were actually going to act upon.

They were continuing to brew and the feedback they were getting was always incredibly positive. Anyone who tried their beer was quick to point out that they had the real potential to have a winner on their hands if they elected to go into business selling the beers they were creating.

Part of their evolving plan was their company name. Like any new business, it's always a struggle to get the perfect name, especially when you need multiple individuals to agree. Tony and Mason had a full page of potential names but nothing was really standing out. Early on, they had thought about the Tulsa Brewing Company, but some research led them to find a now defunct brewpub had already utilized that name. They didn't want to cause any confusion with consumers who might remember the shuttered business, so they decided to keep researching.

The perfect name ended up coming to the duo in an unusual way. Tony was back at home in Kansas visiting his parents. His father had him working with his brother-in-law on a project on their 10+ acres of land. They were moving some lumber when they came across a dead armadillo in the usual "dead armadillo pose" of being on its back, "toots up."

Soon, the beer-fueled brother-in-laws were laughing and joking about the dead armadillo they found, even creating a song about it. Then it hit Tony: Dead Armadillo. It was the perfect name to use for the brewery he and Mason were working on.

He started working on a logo with an upside down armadillo with an x where his eye would have been (he's dead, after all). Mason liked what he was doing and suggested putting a yellow diamond behind the dead critter to give it a "highway sign feel" since that's where you see most dead armadillos, and they knew they had something.

Not only was it fun, it was functional. People would remember the name and the black-and-gold contrast of the logo would stand out on a tap handle. Tony and Mason always thought this should be a major objective for the corporate identity. The duo always despised looking at a tap wall and not being able to pick out what any of the beers were.

Still, despite the branding being resolved, it didn't seem as though the two would actually pursue moving forward with their business. That all changed in 2012 when an individual who had tried their beer convinced them to participate in the Wild Brew, a major fundraiser in Tulsa which attracts thousands of people who come by for live entertainment and to sample beer from local breweries and items from the menu of local restaurants.

The tandem brewed like they never had before in preparation for the event. Response was overwhelming. Attendees began *demanding* the two go into business. The beer and the branding really connected with the people who came by their booth. They then started a Facebook page, and it immediately blew up. They really knew they were onto something by the time they started a website and their t-shirts began moving briskly.

From that point forward the two have been on fast forward.

They immediately began formalizing the casual plan they had been working on for so long. They knew they didn't have the capital to begin a brewery on their own so they sought out a partner to rent them space to use to brew onsite. They ended up finding a company about an hour-and-a-half from Tulsa who would give them time on their equipment to brew their Dead Armadillo beer.

Starting their company was simply like hitting a "Go" button as the demand quickly took off. People truly loved the beer they were brewing, and the dead armadillo is off the charts as an attention grabber with customers. At live events, it's not uncommon for the team to spend as much time selling t-shirts as they are serving up beers. People love to go home wearing a t-shirt with an upside down "x-eyed" armadillo on it.

Recent developments might mean Tony and Mason will be able to seize the moment for a pent up demand for their craft beer. They have struggled with capacity issues not having their own facility. They are currently in the final stages of locking in a building not far from downtown Tulsa. If they are able to close the deal, they will finally have their own production facility. This will rid them of the inconvenience of those 3 hour roundtrip drives, and they will be able to offer tours and tastings as well.

Even though their history is short, Tony and Mason know when they get the type of personal connection they will have during a visit to their brewery it will likely translate into solid merchandise sales as well. Merchandising is great because it generates a revenue stream, each t-shirt become a walking billboard for their product.

Of course, these are two people who know a little about the value of field marketing. After all, every upside armadillo on the side of the highway is an advertisement for their company!

Dead Armadillo Craft Brewing Photo Album

Mason Beercroft and Tony Peck modeling some of Dead Armadillo's most popular shirts

Cans of Dead Armadillo

Those tap handles do stand out!

Dead Armadillo banner

Mason and Tony at an event

Ummmm… cheers?

Dead Armadillo product lineup

Chapter 7
Epic Ales

EPICALES

every possibility is conceivable

3201 1st Avenue South, Suite 104
Seattle, WA 98134
(206) 351-3637

epicales.com
epicales@gmail.com

Established
2009

Leadership
Cody Morris, Brewer and Co-Owner
Travis Kukull, Chef and Co-Owner

"Competition is good. Having a lot of craft breweries around pushes you to do better."
    -Cody Morris

A college hobby turned out to be a career for Cody Morris. A Seattle, Washington, resident, he was attending Evergreen State College in Olympia, Washington, where he was studying philosophy. Not trying to get too existential, but Cody didn't think a career in the field of philosophy was the path he wanted to follow after graduation.

Instead, the hobby he had taken up, brewing his own beer, was something he thought might be an interesting way to earn a living. The philosopher turned would-be beer brewer had difficulty finding a job, though. He applied at many of the local craft brewers found in the Seattle area but no one would give him a chance.

He ended up taking a job at a home brew store. Yes, he had settled instead of truly following his career path, but at least he was in the beer business, albeit peripherally. After about two years, he left the home brew store and went to work for a wine shop.

Spending time at the wine shop opened him up to a new world and served as a nice enhancement to the knowledge base he had acquired about brewing beer. His expertise in home brewing beer translated well to understanding how to make wine. What he was able to add to his repertoire was an understanding of the pairing of wines with foods to enhance a dining experience.

He loved that aspect of the job so much he began working on a plan to start a business consulting restaurants on the pairing of craft beers with the right food dishes. The artistry of craft brewers was so great, the beer they were producing was becoming more and more conducive to the same treatment wine received at so many restaurants with the sommelier (wine steward/expert) many have on hand. Cody felt there was a real opportunity to ratchet up the beer offerings at restaurants by bringing his knowledge and expertise to them.

Owning a consulting business didn't have the feel of freedom you get from owning your own business. After all, you aren't free of having a boss. Each account you work with becomes your boss.

Instead of his consulting idea, Cody decided to go back to his dream of brewing beer. He opened up a tiny space in the SoDo neighborhood of Seattle and began brewing with a single barrel system.

Looking back, he admits it wasn't a plan well thought out. It was a largely industrial area. He didn't have a tasting room, and he was only open one day a week and doing onsite direct sales and distribution.

Still, if you have a good product, often an audience will find you. Cody's beer always received rave reviews from his customers and he started building up a decent client base, even with all of the obstacles he faced with his storefront in SoDo.

When he was introduced to Travis Kukull, they began to discuss the idea of expanding the business to include a restaurant. Travis had worked as a chef across the U.S. in high-end restaurants. He brought skills including French technique cooking and an expertise in Indonesian and Japanese foods.

Together, they expanded the business to include Gastropod, a 38 seat restaurant and bar. Gastropod has a full menu of contemporary food which changes weekly and features 12 taps which includes the complete Epic Ales lineup and a few guest taps of other local craft brewers.

In addition to the change in Epic's business, the SoDo neighborhood has quickly evolved as well. In the five years Cody has been there, it has gone from heavy industrial to a light industrial area. While he was one of the first craft brewers to move into SoDo, the area now has 7 brewers and 8 distillers.

You may wonder about the impact of all of the competition on Cody's business. Well, it's been great. The increased number of brewers and distillers brings customers to the area. Plus, he has a great personal relationship with his fellow craft brewers. Often, they will help one another with machinery, raw ingredients or simply advice. Sure, they compete against each other for customers' spend, but Cody is quick to note, they get to enjoy a friendly relationship, and they let their distributors fight it out over shelf space.

In addition to standout flavors, Cody separates his beer on retailer's shelves with some great label designs from local artists. He has enjoyed good luck over the years in securing artists to take a turn being featured on one of his products by reaching out directly to them. He has found the appeal of being featured on a bottle to be enticing enough that most are willing to work with him on a design.

Even though Cody has now added a three-barrel system to his existing one barrel system, his production capability beyond what is needed for the Gastropod has been pretty limited. Having a relationship with a distributor does have its advantages for him, though.

First of all, it is a revenue stream. While he makes less profit over the taps in his restaurant, he is still generating income from the 10 – 30 cases a week of beer he sells to his distributor.

Secondly, it affords him the luxury of being able to offer the freshest beer possible to his Gastropod customers. If he wasn't selling the bottled beer to his distributor, he would be selling it in the restaurant and his quality would suffer.

Finally, each beer sold through a retailer is an advertisement for his restaurant. If someone enjoys his beer in their home they will be more likely to visit him and enjoy the experience at Gastropod.

You probably couldn't call Cody a planner as a young man. After all, he didn't follow the career path he had studied, and he started his brewery before quickly realizing he needed a different model to be successful.

The Cody of today is completely different, though. He is actively planning for the future and looking ahead to the next step. While he plans to maintain his presence with the Gastropod/brewery in SoDo, he has his mind set on a 7 – 16 barrel brewhouse as an addition to his business portfolio. The plan calls for a 60 – 80 seat dining room and would feature a casual dining experience.

He plans to mix up his beer offerings by playing to the strengths of each brewhouse and brewing beers which will pair well for the featured menu. The increased production will also expand his presence on retailers' shelves. He envisions a long-term goal of expanding in Seattle and Washington and then moving into Oregon, as well. He also has some strong personal connections in both Canada and Japan. They have expressed an interest in importing his beers, so it is highly likely he will be selling his product there in the not too distant future.

Cody maintains a fun approach to his life in the beer business. After all, he will tell you that you never know if you are actually right with beer when you start brewing a batch until about two weeks later.

That will keep you humble!

When Cody began to look into coming up with a name for his craft brewing company, the name Epic stood out to him because he had heard "epic" stood for "every possibility is conceivable." He's used it not only as a name but as the backbone of the company. It makes sense that a philosophy major would have a core value driven by a philosophical approach.

Of course, under the guidance of Cody Morris and his partnership with Travis Kukull, it would appear that every possibility is not only conceivable, it is coming true.

Epic Ales Photo Album

Cody Morris and Travis Kukull

Outside Gastropod

Raw ingredients

The taps at gastropod

Gastropod's logo

Inside Gastropod

EPIC ALES Presents
Huckleberry Sour

1 pt, 6 fl oz
(650 ml)

5.2% ALC/VOL
5 IBUs

Ale brewed huckleberries
aged in oak barrels

Tart, funky, woody and fruity. This sour ale
has fresh huckleberries, malted barley and hops
it was fermented with our own blend of little
critters. Drink now or age.   Batch No.

Brewed and Bottled by Epic Ales LLC, Seattle, Wa
www.epicales.com

GOVERNMENT WARNING: (1) ACCORDING TO THE SURGEON GENERAL, WOMEN
SHOULD NOT DRINK ALCOHOLIC BEVERAGES DURING PREGNANCY BECAUSE OF
THE RISK OF BIRTH DEFECTS. (2) CONSUMPTION OF ALCOHOLIC BEVERAGES
IMPAIRS YOUR ABILITY TO DRIVE A CAR OR OPERATE MACHINERY, AND MAY
CAUSE HEALTH PROBLEMS.

Made in Washington
Please Recycle

Bottle Conditioned. Sediment will develop.
Unfiltered, lively and complex.

EPIC ALES Presents
Interesting Picture of Animals Ale

7.5% ALC/VOL
60 IBUs

1 pt, 6 fl oz
(650 ml)

It seems everyone is making an IPA these
days. We decided to it was time to make
a hoppy ale and come up with a new
meaning of the beloved acronymed ale.
Tweet us your favorite @epicales we'll
use the best and share some brew with you.
Bottle Conditioned. Sediment will develop.
Unfiltered, lively and complex.

We have a pub! www.gastropodsodo.com

Brewed and Bottled by Epic Ales LLC, Seattle, Wa
www.epicales.com

Made in Washington
Please Recycle

1 pt, 6 fl oz
(650 ml)

5% ALC/VOL
5 IBUs

EPIC ALES Presents
OLD WAREHOUSE

American Wild Ale aged
in wine barrels

Wildly fermented then aged in a used
wine barrel, get ready for the tart,
funky and bizarre terrior of SoDo. We
made this with just malted barley and
hops.
Drink now, or age for decades.

Bottle Conditioned. Sediment will develop.
Unfiltered, lively and complex.

Brewed and Bottled by Epic Ales LLC, Seattle, Wa
www.epicales.com

Batch:

Made in Washington
Please Recycle

EPIC ALES Presents
Salty Ghosts

1 pt, 6 fl oz
(650 ml)

4.2% ALC/VOL
10 IBUs

American Wild Ale
brewed with coriander and sea salt

This sour ale is a gose, an obscure traditional
German brew. Made with wheat, barley, sea salt,
coriander and hops. It is tart and refreshing
with a unique savory mouthfeel and finish.

Prost!

Bottle Conditioned. Sediment will develop.
Unfiltered, lively and complex. Pour Slowly.
We have a pub! www.gastropodsodo.com

Brewed and Bottled by Epic Ales LLC, Seattle, Wa
www.epicales.com

Batch No.

Made in Washington
Please Recycle

Epic Ales product lineup

Chapter 8
Foothills Brewing

Brewery: 3800 Kimwell Drive, Winston-Salem, NC 27103
Brewpub: 638 W. 4th Street, Winston-Salem, NC 27101
(336) 777-3348

foothillsbrewing.com
hello@foothillsbrewing.com

Established
2005

Leadership
Jamie Bartholomaus, President and Brewmaster
Matt Masten, Co-Owner

"I brewed my first beer at the age of 18. That seems young, but I was already a sophomore in college. I have a late birthday."
       -Jamie Bartholomaus

With a homebrewing hobby that started at the age of 18, you might think Jamie Bartholomaus was on a single track for his career. Well, with the benefit of hindsight, it is true he may have been destined to be in the beer business, but it wasn't always a foregone conclusion it would be what he would do for a living.

While he worked at brewpubs on the brewing side throughout his college years at the University of Georgia, Jamie studied anthropology. "Oh, okay," you are probably thinking, "Jamie studied anthropology in college but fell back on beer when he couldn't find work in the field after graduation."

Not true.

Jamie did, in fact, land a job in anthropology after graduation. The caveat needs to be stated that anthropology is traditionally a low-paying field. As such, Jamie continued to supplement his income even when he was working in the anthropology field by working secondary at brewpubs to help make ends meet.

The reason Jamie switched career paths wasn't lack of job options; it was the lifestyle associated with the job. First of all, the job isn't what most people conjure up in their minds when they think of what an anthropologist does. Most working anthropologists aren't gently sweeping off dinosaur bones from exotic locations or working sites surrounding the Great Pyramids.

Most anthropologists are employed by the government. The primary function of these individuals is to go into areas which haven't been developed yet to check the area to see if it has any historical or cultural significance buried under years of soil and overgrowth. Jamie cites a reservoir area near Macon, Georgia, as an example of a site he worked on. It had been the home of a historic Native American village. Artifacts were unearthed, cataloged and boxed up. A few bodies were uncovered which were turned over to Native American tribes in the area.

While Jamie did enjoy the work, the "gypsy lifestyle" of moving around frequently, not making much money, and only working with the same eight people every day got to be a drag. Jamie ended up leaving the industry and concentrated full-time on making it in the beer business.

He went to work for a craft brewery. He liked the product they produced and the owners, but they weren't into expanding their brand. They seemed content with the success they had achieved and weren't looking to stretch themselves as an organization to try to build the brand beyond the world of being a small local player.

Friends and family knew he was looking to do more in the business and perhaps looking at starting his own place at some point. One day a friend told him he knew of a group of investors who were looking to open a brewery in Winston-Salem, North Carolina. Jamie reached out to them and joined the group.

Working with a group provided challenges in getting everyone to agree on decisions like naming the company. Jamie likes to say that the one thing everyone had to agree on was their address was 638, so they used 638 Brewing Company which would serve as the parent for their brewpub and later their production brewery. Ultimately, they chose

Foothills Brewing as a tribute to the area at the foothills of the Blue Ridge and Great Smoky Mountains.

Getting a logo for their company was also an early challenge. They felt their graphic designer kept coming up with beer label ideas when they were looking to first establish a corporate identity with a logo. When they clarified exactly what they were looking for, their graphic artist was able to produce not only a great company logo, but also has been able to establish the company identity for them through their unique and highly artistic labels and promotional material.

Jamie laughs now when he reflects on the fact the amount the company spent for the corporate logo along with the labels for their five initial beers is about what they now spend monthly with their design firm.

He's joking, of course, but the reason they spend so much is the fact the company's branding touches every facet of Foothill Brewery's business (website, cars, promotional material, letterhead, schwag, etc.). Jamie quickly notes that despite the large expense of their brand identity, it's extremely valuable in helping accomplish their goal of being a regional brand along the corridor between Washington, D.C. and Atlanta, Georgia.

The company's Hoppyum IPA is their most popular beer in terms of cases sold, but truth be told, their most "popular beer" is clearly their Russian Imperial Stout they call Sexual Chocolate. Many companies offer seasonal beers which tie into different holidays (Christmas and Halloween being two of the most popular). Jamie thought a chocolate beer would be perfect for Valentine's Day, and it has been an unbelievable success. Sexual Chocolate is amongst the rarest of the beers in that it truly is an "event beer." People literally camp out to buy it. Let's not forget, Valentine's Day is in February, not the time of the year most conducive to spending the night on the street in a folding chair. Still, around 300 – 400 people spend a night outside just to ensure they get their yearly taste of Sexual Chocolate!

Beer isn't Jamie's only passion when it comes to the world of beverages. He and his wife Sarah also enjoy roasting their own coffee. Over the years they have refined their process, and Jamie points out they can create a pretty tasty blend at this point. While he's not getting into the coffee business, it wouldn't be surprising to see some of their roasted coffee to be married into one of their beers at some point.

In 2010, the company expanded beyond their brewpub by leasing a building for their production brewery. It took them about a year to build it out, but they have been producing most of their beer at the new facility since 2011.

Currently, the company is in the process of buying the building which houses their production brewery. Once the sale is complete, they plan to remodel the facility to cater to individuals visiting. They envision the remodeled facility to be a place where individuals can be introduced to their product through tours and enjoy their favorites in a taproom.

Despite the success of their brewpub in downtown Winston-Salem, Jamie keeps his management to the brewery side. He readily acknowledges he likes to leave the food side of owning a restaurant to his team to have the true expertise in the area.

The growth of their brand has been impressive. They are up 78% this year versus the previous year in which they managed to grow their business 110%.

This explosive growth does cause its own set of challenges, growing pains if you will, but these are the sort of problems any owner would gladly like to take on.

Long-term, Jamie foresees expansion to Georgia (the next market beyond their current 300-mile swath of real estate they want to be known in) and Pennsylvania since Jamie grew up there. Those expansions would be well down the road, though.

After all, anthropologist Jamie is still digging up opportunities in his own backyard!

Foothills Brewing Photo Album

Jamie Bartholomaus

Foothills Brewing

The Foothills' truck

A Foothills' growler

The Foothills' car

Pouring a beer

Label detail

Foothills Brewery product lineup

Chapter 9
Fordham & Dominion Brewing Company

FORDHAM&DOMINION

B R E W I N G • C O M P A N Y

1284 McD Drive
Dover, DE 19901
(302) 678-4810

fordhamanddominion.com

Established
1989

Leadership
Jim Lutz, President and CEO

"Our roots run deep throughout the Mid-Atlantic region and we remain dedicated to our craft."
  -Jim Lutz

A beer man.

It's safe to say it's an appropriate moniker for Jim Lutz. After all, he's spent his entire career in the beer business. He grew up in Wisconsin, and he crisscrossed the country also living in Arizona and Colorado prior to settling into Maryland, where he still lives today.

Along the way he only worked in the beer industry, going all the way back to his first job back in Wisconsin at Pabst. Each move was for a new opportunity in the beer business though his primary responsibility at each of his jobs in the industry was tied to sales and marketing.

His success in the industry led him to some consulting work. It was via the consulting he was doing with Fordham Brewery in Annapolis, Maryland, where he was introduced to the company he would one day be running.

The first part of the Fordham & Dominion story starts in 1989 with Jerry Bailey, a federal government employee who got tired of his job and started Old Dominion Brewery (named after the nickname of Virginia). By 1995, the company had risen to one of the top 50 craft breweries in the United States. Their flagship beer was an Oak Barrel Stout made with oak chips and vanilla beans.

The year 1995 was also a milestone year for what was ultimately to become the second half of the company. Fordham Brewing was opened in a brewpub called Ram's Head Restaurant in Annapolis, Maryland, that year. The name came from Benjamin Fordham who had successfully petitioned Queen Anne to charter a brewery in the United States in 1703.

Unlike the craft-style unique beers Old Dominion was known for, Fordham was brewing easy-drinking German style beers. Both companies continued their success independently of each other until a series of non-related events would bring them together.

The first happened with Fordham. By 2003, they had maxed out capacity at their existing facility. With no further ability to grow their business at their current location, they began to look at companies to buy out to continue the upward trajectory they had been on prior to reaching their capacity limits.

Back in Ashburn, Virginia, Jerry Bailey was looking to retire from his successful brewery. Eventually, the two companies would join forces, each fulfilling the need of the other (Fordham bought out Old Dominion meaning Jerry could retire, and they could not only reap the benefits of additional capacity, they also were picking up another brand which was doing well in its own right).

At first, the two companies were run totally separate, each staying in its original location. By 2009, to maximize efficiencies of running two companies, along with the need for increased capacity, the two companies were joined together at a new facility in Dover, Delaware. The goal was to have both companies each retain their unique identity and specialties but back office functions could be combined under a parent company/subsidiary format.

In 2011, Jim Lutz was brought in from his consultant role as an owner and to serve as the president and CEO. His photo on the company website lists him as "President and Forklift Driver" which is actually true. Jim is a hands-on owner and literally gets involved in every facet of the business from running the bottling line to inventory management to making sales calls to establishing company vision and direction.

Their long-term goals remain modest and achievable. Their goal is to stay within 150 miles of their facility in Dover. This gives them access to Maryland, Virginia, D.C., Pennsylvania, New Jersey and Delaware. They only have two exceptions to this plan: Michigan and London. They have owners who live in these locations so they want to ensure they can buy a Fordham & Dominion beer at the stores near their houses.

Owning a beer company is awesome!

The reason they stick to their 150 miles radius sans those two exceptions is the fact they believe their beer is best enjoyed as fresh as possible. They only way they are able to commit to that level of freshness to their customers is to limit the time in transit and at warehouses awaiting shipping to distributors.

Their main focus for the moment is to grow their business in their backyard, literally. Delaware is the key area where they want to penetrate further. It sounds crazy that a brewery would need to grow their business in their home state, but don't forget, Delaware is their adopted home state. It's still early in their time there, and they look to continue to make inroads across the state in the near future.

A visit to their brewery in Dover answers a lot of questions as to why Fordham & Dominion stands out above its competition. It's the people. Visitors get a feel for just how much fun it is to work at the brewery with a visit. Sites like Yelp are loaded with customers' reviews talking about how much fun it is and all of the great laughs they enjoyed during their tours.

The fun doesn't stop with just interaction with visitors. Each employee has a key job in the process for getting their beers to market. Whether it's management like Jim Lutz, the brewers who make the beer, the marketing department who establish the character and story for each offering or the sales team who sell their product at market level, each person's role must be done with precision and perfection to make it happen.

Precision and perfection are two things that happen quite a lot at Fordham & Dominion!

Fordham & Dominion Brewing Company Photo Album

Jim Lutz

"Cans" of beer

Events are one of the most popular way Fordham & Dominion connects with its customers

Some of the team working an event

The company is also known for its handcrafted sodas

FORDHAM

RINSE & REPEAT SERIES
BEER SOAP
4.25 OZ. NT WT

They even have a beer soap!

Even though they are owned by the same parent company, Fordham and Dominion each have their own company logo as well as their own unique identity.

Samples of some of the company's posters/artwork

Fordham & Dominion product lineup

Chapter 10
Full Sail Brewing

408 Columbia Street
Hood River, OR 97031
(541) 386-7316

fullsailbrewing.com

Established
1987

Leadership
Irene Firmat, Founder & CEO

"How can you not walk away from a visit to a biergarten in Munich and not think, life is better with beer?"
        -Irene Firmat

Irene Firmat understands the importance beer can play in the lives of people.

It's true.

She may have a better understanding of this concept than anyone else you will ever meet in your life. Sure, part of her knowledge clearly comes from the fact she has been able to start a craft brewing company which has managed to not only survive in a very competitive field, but thrive.

Best of all, her company has mirrored the ideals of the woman herself. One of the most rewarding aspects of building Full Sail Brewing is the fact she has created a company where workers are respected for what they bring to the company. They have a culture where individuals can thrive and bring their very best to the job every day because they have a great environment to work in.

She has managed to build the company in this model with the simple approach of treating her employees with respect and, ultimately, turning it over to them via an employee-ownership structure. In-turn, customers of Full Sail Brewing often point out how well they are treated by the staff. When each employee is an employee-owner, understanding how every customer is the reason for them being there, makes it's easy to see how the corporate structure and its employees leads to success.

Irene's understanding of the role beer plays in society goes beyond everything positive which has happened with her company. For her, it's also personal. When the brewer she hired to launch the company left the organization, she began an extensive search for his replacement. One candidate, Jamie Emmerson, seemed the perfect fit. He had his Masters in Brewing Science and his undergrad work had been in organic chemistry. To top it off, he had even spent a year in Munich where he got to immerse himself in the local beer scene.

Not only was Jamie hired, but soon he and Irene fell in love and were married. Today, they have been married more than 25 years, and Irene notes that while wine gets all the credit as the beverage of choice in romance, beer is way more romantic!

Despite the positive impact beer has had on her personal and professional life, Irene's knowledge about the importance of beer in society goes even deeper still. It has been a guiding philosophy to her success.

After backpacking across Europe and witnessing firsthand the positive impact beer had on the local communities, Irene had a deep understanding of the relevance of beer. Business was conducted over a mug of beer, or people would rehash what was going on in their lives. Others were making memories with friends by going out and celebrating while enjoying a few tankards.

It would be this understanding which would drive Irene in the decisions she made to set the direction of the company. In doing so, she's managed to avoid the trends and following "what's hot" at the time to chase more beer sales. Instead of raising the bar in what she calls the "hops wars" with beers that having a continued increase in alcohol content, Full Sail Brewing has stayed the course of offering traditional beers. Product offerings where a group can enjoy a beer and start thinking about the next one as soon as they take a drink, something you aren't doing with alcohol contents 9% and higher with some of the trendy offerings which can be found now.

The experience remains about the friends and the moment over the alcohol. This core approach is the understanding Irene has about beer and truly has been the greatest driving force in the company's success.

Getting to this point was certainly unconventional to say the least. After the previously mentioned backpack trip across Europe, Irene settled back into her home state of New York, working in retail in a department store. She went out to Oregon to visit a college friend and fell in love with the area.

Being young and without a family, mortgage or a job which would tie her down, she decided to pick up and move west to live. She got a job working as a department store buyer which turned out to be great for her at the time since it meant she would have to travel back home to New York frequently for buying trips.

Over time, she became disillusioned with working for a publicly-held company. The organization was so beholden to earnings reports, they would often do things which clearly were not best for the organization for the long term, but helped the quarterly reporting of earning statements.

She knew the best approach for her was going to be owning her own business. She began to search for opportunities. One area she honed in on was beer. While it's hard to believe now, in 1984 there was a shortage of companies offering bottled beer at retail. As an avid beer drinker and with the previously mentioned deeper understanding of the impact of beer as an agent of a strong sense of community, she decided to open a brewery.

The challenges of opening a brewery in 1984 went beyond just funding. Getting information was almost impossible. Even licensing was a struggle. This wasn't because the individuals she was working with weren't helpful, it's because licensing a brewery wasn't something they did. It had been 40 or 50 years since they had been actively licensing breweries in Oregon. As such, a whole new generation of individuals were trying to figure out how to license the new breweries popping up while Irene was trying to figure out how to start her business.

One of the best stories Irene has comes from the very process of licensing her business. Initially, she had come up with the name Sasquatch Brewing for the company. Another established brewery had a beer line they called Bigfoot, and they quickly sent Irene a cease and desist letter.

This sent her back to the drawing board and she was struggling to come up with a new name. One of the employees at the licensing office suggested a name he had checked to be clear: Full Sail Brewing. As soon as she heard it, Irene was hooked. It was perfect. They were right on the Columbia River Gorge. Sailing was a popular hobby there. Logo design would be simple.

It had taken three years of research, paperwork and licensing but Full Sail Brewing was officially in business on September 27, 1987!

For Irene and her perfectionist mantra, the beer had to be just right. Irene was steadfast in her desire to have a balanced product. She didn't want it "too hoppy, too malty or too roasty" as she says. Imbalanced beers make it too much about those single ingredients, and you miss the complexity of the beers. Instead of tasting the next layer, you are focused on that one aspect which ruins the experience of enjoying the beer.

Once they perfected their recipe, there were still challenges. The first year was difficult. They only managed 287 barrels of production. Still, there were wins and milestones. Irene laughs when she shares a tidbit the first time she saw her beer on the shelf in a grocery store. She was so stunned, she almost wrecked her car when she drove over the center divider in the parking lot leaving the store!

As their brand began to grow, Irene has maintained her focus on the quality of their beer to the path of continued growth. Under her guidance, the company has avoided the bizarre ingredients, frat boyish advertising and promotion and gimmicks many of her competitors utilized.

Instead she continues her quest to find the perfect balanced beer. The offering which serves as the perfect backdrop to conversations, family, friends and fun. That doesn't mean the company doesn't continue to innovate and evolve.

They do.

In fact, Full Sail Brewing is often at the forefront of innovation and new offerings in craft brewing. They just take the approach of not chasing the latest and greatest.

Instead, they are trying to perfect the best offerings utilizing the core ingredients of hops, malt, yeast and water. Under the guidance of Irene Firmat, it's highly likely her team of employee-owners will find as close to beer perfection as anyone has managed to create.

Full Sail ahead!

Full Sail Brewing Photo Album

Irene Firmat

Jamie Emmerson

Packaging on the production line

Ready to ship

The front of Full Sail Brewing

View of Mount Hood

The Full Sail team

Full Sail Brewing product lineup

Chapter 11
Great Northern Brewing Company

2 Central Avenue, Suite 1
Whitefish, MT
(406) 863-1000

greatnorthernbrewing.com
brewmaster@greatnorthernbrewing.com

Established
1995

Leadership
Joe Barberis, Head Brewer
Marcus Duffey, General Manager

"We recently expanded our production capabilities by 150% and we're already at full production of our new capacity."
-Joe Barberis

Minott Wessinger was just following his family legacy when he launched McKenzie River Corporation in San Francisco in 1987. His great-great grandfather was Henry Weinhard, a pioneer in brewing in the Pacific Northwest. Mr. Weinhard began brewing in Portland in the 1850s and would launch a brewery which would stay in business until the 1990s.

Minott's McKenzie River Corporation would develop multiple brands in several lines of the beverage industry. (In addition to beer he would also have sparkling water, distilled spirits and energy drink lines).

In 1994, he hired respected architect Joe Esherick, who designed the famed Monterey Bay Aquarium amongst his many other works, to build a brewery in Whitefish, Montana. Whitefish, a place where Minott would vacation, was selected for its natural beauty, rugged persona and the fact the quality of its water would be a main ingredient in its beer. The name for the venture was the Great Northern Brewing Company which fit well with both the geography and the tie-in to the fact Whitefish was a railroad town served by the Great Northern Railroad.

The building designed by Joe Esherick is stunning. It is located in downtown Whitefish and framed in the beauty of the area. It's a modern design with a simple layout of metal framing and floor to ceiling windows. At four stories, it is the tallest building in Whitefish, which makes for unbelievable views of the mountains.

The building itself also works its way into the brewing process. Traditional brewing methods employed a gravity-based system to move product through the stages of production. Based out of need, moving hundreds of gallons of liquid was challenging without today's modern pump technology, so early brewers would utilize gravity to do most of the work in moving their beer to different tanks.

While Great Northern has access to technology early brewers could have only hoped for, they have opted to utilize traditional methods employing their own gravity-fed system. This comes from the combination of wanting to employ a traditional German approach to their brewing methods as well as the fact they are landlocked in their facility, and the pumps would take up room they can utilize to produce more beer.

Hmm.

More beer or pumps?

Let's go with the beer!

The end result is a brewing experience which is much more traditional than most breweries employ. This makes for both unique tours and a standout beer. After all, you are seeing a process not often utilized today, and the Great Northern team will tell you the traditional approach to their craft is what makes their beers a cut above their competitors as well.

In the early 2000s, Minott Wessinger began selling off some of his beverage holdings. He divested some of his brands to Pabst and Miller. In 2002 he also sold Great Northern.

Marcus Duffey, who met his wife, a Whitefish, Montana, native while going to college at Gonzaga in Washington, was brought in as a partner to serve as the general manager.

The company, led in production by Head Brewer Joe Barberis, began to expand their product line. The company has five flagship beers they produce year round, multiple seasonals they bring back every year as well as limited releases rotated in-and-out.

Their flagship beers include Wild Huckleberry Wheat Lager. This offering embraces this elusive fruit which is exclusive to the mountainous areas of the Pacific Northwest. The huckleberry is not grown commercially and thus it is harvested by individuals who forage through the mountains to pick the fruit which looks in shape to be similar to blueberries but is darker and tarter than the typical blueberry found at your local grocer. A dedicated and knowledgeable individual might be able to pick five gallons of huckleberries in a day.

As you can imagine, it makes for a challenging and expensive ingredient to utilize for Great Northern. They have a supplier who provides them with the juice of the berry, which they use to produce their "not bitter/not sweet" Wild Huckleberry Wheat Lager. This lager gives a uniquely Whitefish, Montana, drinking experience for the throngs of tourists who come to visit the state in the summer.

Great Northern Brewing Company also has a partnership: a coffee company producing SnowGhost Coffee.

SnowGhost is a limited edition beer the company offers and refers to the unique formations the trees in the area begin to take on as the combination of snow and ice continues to pile on them throughout the long winters. Over time, they begin to look like ghosts on the mountain, particularly when seen through foggy conditions. The partnership with Montana Coffee Traders recreates the essence of the flavor profile of SnowGhost in a coffee blend.

In 2014, Great Northern Brewing Company expanded production from a 40 barrel system to a 100 barrel system. Within months, they had expanded their production to run at full capacity of their new system.

Visitors to the brewery enjoy a fun and informative visit. They get to experience the beauty of the area while witnessing production utilizing traditional German brewing methods. A spiral staircase takes them through the gravity-fed brewing process. At the end of the tour they get to sample all of Great Northern's beers while enjoying unobstructed views of Whitefish.

Kicking back and enjoying a Wild Huckleberry Wheat Lager while taking in the mountains of Whitefish, Montana… that doesn't sound too bad, does it?

Great Northern Brewing Company Photo Album

Joe Barberis (working)

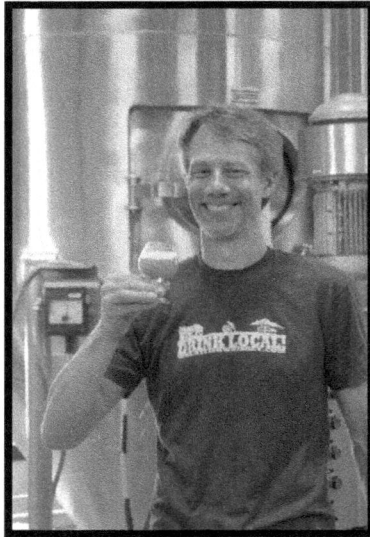

Joe Barberis (also working… he is a brewmaster after all!)

Great Northern's building in downtown Whitefish

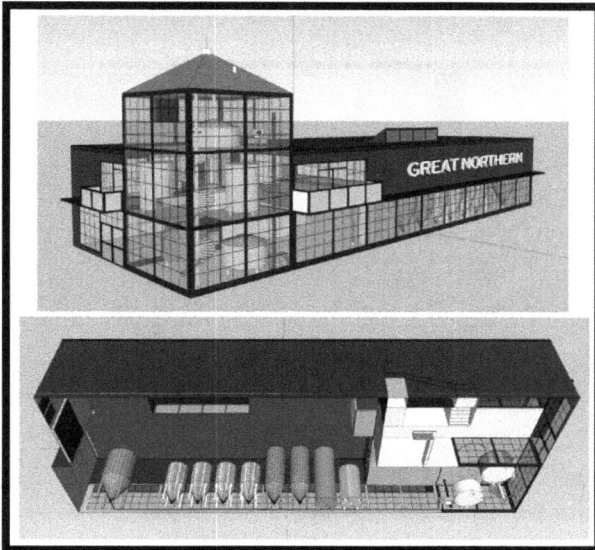
The plans, showing the full details of the brewery

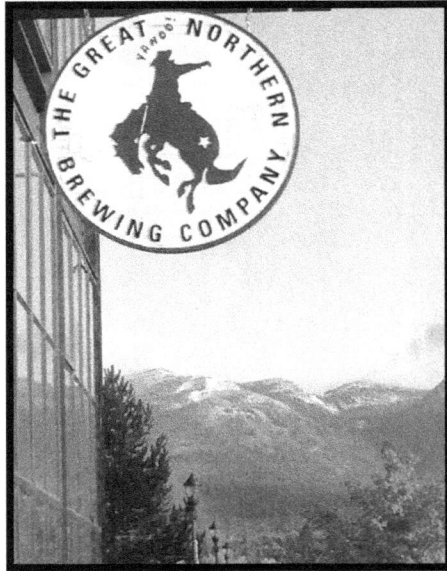

The view from the brewery is spectacular

Pint glasses ready to go

Working up a thirst for a beer

Hops

Great Northern's packaging is bold and beautiful

Great Northern's product lineup

Chapter 12
Heavy Seas Beer

4615 Hollins Ferry Road
Halethorpe, MD 21227
(410) 247-7822

hsbeer.com

Established
1995

Leadership
Hugh Sisson, Founder

"I worked in theatre after graduation, but soon the romance of poverty had grown thin."
-Hugh Sisson

With so many in the craft beer industry, brewing is a lifelong passion. The allure of bringing an artistry to hops, yeast and water starts early (usually after some positive college experiences). Interest in starting a brewery are hashed and rehashed over the homebrews created by the potential proprietor. Finally, the plan takes effect when an actual business is started.

For Hugh Sisson, the script worked out a little differently. He was a double major in college studying English and Theatre. After obtaining his undergraduate degree, he began living his dream by working in theatre. Even as he went back to school to get his graduate degree, he continued to pursue work in the acting field.

By the time he completed graduate school, he still hoped to make it in acting, but the appeal of actually having money meant he would need to find a steady job. His father had opened a bar called Sisson's in 1979 and had often floated the idea to Hugh about working there. Hugh didn't like the thought of working at the bar while continuing to pursue acting and directing work. He came around when he finally woke up to the fact most struggling actors either tend bar or wait tables. It seemed like he might as well help his father out rather than work somewhere else.

As Hugh took charge of running the bar, he wanted to do something to make it stand out. His idea was to go with a beer joint theme, which in 1982 was pretty bold. There weren't the plethora of craft breweries to choose from, so they ended up offering a lot of imports at the bar.

Also around this time, Hugh began crafting beer at his house. His home brewing went beyond simply wanting to enjoy a few suds at home. He utilized the knowledge he was gaining to assist his efforts in expanding his range of beer offered by learning about ingredients and different brewing styles.

As the concept of brewpubs started picking up around the country, Hugh's father decided to look into the idea of bringing it to Sisson's. When they inquired to the State of Maryland, they found it wasn't legal to operate a brewpub in Maryland. Hugh and his father began working with State Senator George Della, Jr. to lobby for a bill which would legalize brewpubs.

In 1988, their efforts were successful, and their bill was signed into law. So much of Hugh and his father's efforts had been into getting their quest legalized, so when it became a reality, they realized they had a lot of work to do. They scrambled to get up to speed on running a craft brewpub so they could ensure they were the first in the business they had worked so hard to get legalized.

In 1989, their dream was realized, and Sisson's became Maryland's first brewpub with Hugh as the head brewer. Father and son continued to grow the family business through the mid-90s.

In 1995, Hugh left the family business to start his own business, a production brewery called Clipper City. While craft brewers had been on the rise when Hugh was developing his business plan (showing growth year over year in the 40, 60 or even 70 percent range each year… though those numbers were on a very small base as craft brewing was truly just getting started back then), by 1996, the numbers had fallen flat.

In 1997, Hugh began to contract brewing for other beer companies to help pay the bills. Ultimately, this would save his company and allow him to stay in business during these lean times.

As cash began to flow back into the coffers, Hugh was able to purchase a competitor called Oxford. He continued to run it as a second brand with the hope of gaining market share by having two brands.

Drawing upon his experience in the world of acting, Hugh was very familiar with the concept of a "breakout star." A breakout star in the acting world would be someone with a bit part who becomes popular with the audiences and in turn takes on a larger role because of said popularity. In 2004, he was about to have his own experience with this concept as he looked to add another line of specialty beers under the name Heavy Seas.

Right away beer drinkers took to the name. They also identified with the pirate theme and logo the brand had. At the same time he was recognizing issues with his other brands.

His original beer, Clipper City was named based on the fact his hometown of Baltimore was the place where the first clipper ships were designed and built. He had hoped naming it after something so deeply-rooted in the history of his homebase he would generate a passion for his product.

The only problem being it was too "deeply-rooted" in the past. Though he had the knowledge the clipper ship was created in Baltimore, he was amazed to find out most people in the area didn't know that little nugget. Rather than giving it a hometown feel, people weren't responsive to it… or worse yet, they thought it was a domestic beer from another city.

Facing the notion people didn't have a passion for the name Clipper City, heightened by the fact consumers were confused by having beers under three names, in 2010 Hugh decided to brew all of his products under the Heavy Seas name.

Unfortunately for Hugh, this didn't end his naming woes. An issue popped up when they were looking to launch a new beer under their Heavy Seas brand. They had gone through the entire process of confirming the availability of a name. Just when they were ready to commit, they found a small brewer already using the name. The brewery owner had never gone through the proper channels to protect the name himself so, technically, Heavy Seas could use it.

Still, it didn't seem right for Hugh to just move forward without asking. They contacted the brewery owner and during their initial call he agreed to let Hugh use the name so long as he didn't sell it in his market.

Done deal!

Not so fast, though. The other brewer spoke to his attorney and decided there would need to be some compensation to use the name. Hugh declined, but it left him without a name for his new beer. Then it just popped in his head: Loose Cannon.

Perfect!

Loose Cannon quickly became Heavy Seas best selling beer, and today accounts for over 50% of the company's business. While the beer stands on its own, Hugh does attribute a lot of the initial success in getting consumers to try based on the name. Loose Cannon is the perfect name for a beer, and it has served the company well.

Even in his acting days, Hugh Sisson never came across a script which read like his real life. If he had, he would have passed on the role. It just doesn't seem plausible.

Think about it…

A would-be actor decides to become a bartender. He changes the approach for the operation from a full-service bar to focus exclusively on beer. It leads to his interest in craft brewing. He helps get his home state laws changed so he can open a brewpub. He launches his own beer brand. The beer company struggles initially, but he rights the ship by changing its ship-themed name to one which conjures up images of swashbuckling pirates which he then incorporates into his branding. The business launches into the stratosphere, and he expands his operation from 15,000 square feet to 40,000.

Roll credits.

It has definitely been the part Hugh Sisson was destined to play!

Heavy Seas Beer Photo Album

Hugh Sisson

The perfect pairing with a Heavy Seas beer

Bottle run

Loose Cannon cans, ready to fill

Barrel aging

The tap room

Some of Heavy Seas' awards

Heavy Seas Beer product lineup

Chapter 13
Jester King Brewery

13005 Fitzhugh Road, Bldg. B
Austin, TX 78736
(512) 537-5100

jesterkingbrewery.com
info@jesterkingbrewery.com.com

Established
2010

Leadership
Ron Extract, Co-Owner
Jeffrey Stuffings, Co-Owner
Michael Steffing, Co-Owner

"As long as we continue to find an audience, we will go by the philosophy that we brew what we like to drink."
-Ron Extract

Brothers Jeff Stuffings and Michael Steffing had very different lives. First of all, there was the difference in the names. Michael had changed his last name to reflect the original spelling of the family surname.

Next, there was the matter of the age difference meaning they didn't really grow up together. Their careers were quite different with Jeff being employed as a practicing attorney and Michael working in finance. Finally, they also had a lot of real estate between them as Jeff was in Florida, and Michael was in Colorado.

Add beer to the mix, and all of those differences get cast aside, and a glorious family reunion ensues!

It all started with Jeff's wife. They had met in college, and she was from Texas. Like any good Texan, she wanted to get home. When she and Jeff decided to move there, Jeff was looking for employment. Despite no industry experience beyond his own homebrewing and some time working in a homebrew shop years earlier, Jeff put together a business plan to start a brewery.

As the plan began to take shape, Michael orchestrated a family reunion by deciding to join his brother in business in Texas.

Around the same time Jeff was making his move to Texas, and despite reservations about moving to the Lone Star State, Ron Extract was about to make the move as well. While this led to a lot of both personal and professional questions for him, Ron was following a girlfriend there from Wisconsin.

Ron had a significant background in the beer industry, even serving as an assistant brewer at one point and most recently as a beer importer. Early on he found continuing work in the beer importing business to be difficult with the repressive rules Texas had on the books at the time.

Unlike most states, Texas required the company exporting beer/alcohol to the U.S. to hold the license to ship the product into the state rather than the importing company. This meant companies, like the one Ron worked for, had to try to convince companies outside of the U.S. to pay $3,000 - $6,000 every two years for licenses in the low volume world of craft brewers.

Ron had moved to a part-time role as he looked to get his own small independent distribution company off of the ground. He had been reading about the work brothers Jeff and Michael were doing with their beer company so he contacted them about the new distribution company he was starting.

The three men quickly became friends and with Jeff and Michael, having just lost a third partner they had brought in, there was an opportunity for Ron to get an equity stake and join the organization to help with brewing. Ron joined Jester King Brewery, and the three have been friends and business partners since.

The name Jester King came from the idea the company with the largest market share is known as the "King of Beers." Their small company, being outside of the reign of the king, became the "jesters of the brewing world."

That was how the name got its start, anyway. It began to take on an additional meaning for these "jesters of the brewing world" to enjoy an occasional laugh about. It seems the trio has often received advice telling them they shouldn't be doing some of the things they have done with their business. Despite the fact they haven't followed the advice of some of the veterans of the craft brewing world, the company has continued to thrive.

It sounds like these jesters are outside the reign of everyone in the industry, not just the big players.

Their product was a true farmhouse brand. They use locally sourced malt and grain and have their own water source. They use wild yeasts from their property and ferment the beers onsite in barrels.

Another signature of the company is the constant rotation of product. They continue to experiment and offer new beers for their customers. The driving force behind all of their creativity is to simply create a product they would enjoy drinking. As long as they are making beer they want to drink, they assume their customers are happy, and thus far it's worked out exactly that way.

Besides the fun name and the standout product, another key factor to their success has been graphic artist Josh Cockrell. Josh was working on his own freelance company and started doing a little design work for Jester King Brewery. His work captured the spirit of exactly what Jeff, Michael and Ron were trying to accomplish.

When Josh expressed an interest in joining the company, they weren't quite ready to take on a graphic artist full-time. They did need some help. The deal they worked out was that if Josh was willing to work at the brewery, filling in wherever they needed him, the balance of his schedule could be filled out doing the graphic design work for the company.

Josh agreed to do it, and, as advertised, did a little bit of everything for the company. Whether it was managing the tasting room, delivering kegs or cleaning up after production, Josh was willing to do it. When the time was right, Jeff, Michael and Ron welcomed Josh aboard full-time to the team as a graphic artist. Today, he stays busy providing the imagery supporting what the trio is creating with their craft farmhouse beers.

The future of Jester King Brewery is one of conservative growth. They are not looking to rapidly expand their business. In fact, if they stay exactly where they are in terms of production and distribution, they are actually okay with it.

They have distribution in several stores locally and aren't looking to expand into that area any further right now. Recent changes in the laws of Texas allow them to do more with their customers onsite at their brewery than they ever have. Now, they can not only offer tastings but they can sell packaged beer to their customers, as well. In the foreseeable future, that is the area of growth for Jester King Brewery.

Last year they made 1,000 barrels of beer, and the year before they had made 1,200 barrels. Two-hundred barrels is a significant drop-off from a starting point of 1,200, but it is a source of pride for Jeff, Michael and Ron.

The reason they produced less wasn't a decrease in demand, it was the formulation of even better products. They have slowed their fermentation and begun to offer beers utilizing a process of re-fermentation.

The end result: taking the great beers they already had and upping the ante. That actually sounds about right…

Remember, these are three guys whose driving force behind the decision they make is, "Would we want to drink this?" The fact is they are willing to decrease production to simply make better beers.

Yep.

That sounds about right.

Jester King Brewery Photo Album

Jeffrey Stuffings, Ron Extract and Michael Steffing

The picnic area behind Jester King Brewery

Let's brew some beer!

It's going to be awesome!

Barrel aging beer

Before and after

And now we drink

Jester King Brewery product lineup

Chapter 14
Jolly Pumpkin Artisan Ales

2319 Bishop Circle East
Dexter, MI 48130

jollypumpkin.com
artisanales@gmail.com

Established
2003

Leadership
Ron Jeffries, Founder

"Brewing beer is a craft. From an outsider's perspective a cabinetmaker's job might look like you are doing the exact same thing every day. It's a craft, though. There are interesting challenges the cabinetmaker encounters which makes each day unique. It's the same with beer."
-Ron Jeffries

Ron Jeffries was born in Ann Arbor, Michigan. In college, he met his future wife Laurie at a party. Upon getting married, it seemed they were destined to live the life of musicians. Ron was in a band and spent a lot of time on the road when they were touring.

With plans to start a family, a life crisscrossing the country didn't seem appealing so Ron quit the band to join another group which only played in Michigan. While he had found an ideal situation for a family man, only playing in Michigan really hampered the potential gigs for the band.

The group decided to make a move they collectively felt would provide a happy medium. They would relocate to Western Massachusetts. There was easy access to markets like New York, Boston and Philadelphia. They would be able to tour and play these major metropolitan areas while only being a few hours from home.

Once again their plans didn't work out as well as they had hoped. This time the issue was their home base. They had found themselves in the middle of "Nowhere, Massachusetts." Not exactly a fun or thriving metropolis.

The band members began looking to relocate again. They were wide open to go anywhere so long as they could capture the magic of having large segments of population surrounding them as well as a great place to live in a central location.

Ultimately, Ron notes the band members began to take themselves too seriously. The idea of making a change to launch a big time music career led to infighting and soon the band basically imploded.

Ron decided it was time to move on from the music industry and enrolled again at the University of Michigan in the graduate school program. Even though his undergraduate degree had been in literature, he had always taken science classes as electives. He was now enrolled in the University of Michigan's Masters of Science program.

While working on his degree, he stopped by a friend's house who was brewing some beer. A certified "scientist in the making," Ron was smitten not only with making beer, a product he readily enjoyed, but the science behind it. Just seeing his friend trying to make his inaugural batch of beer got Ron thinking. By the next day, Ron called his buddy and asked him if he wanted to open up a microbrewery.

Time out.

His buddy was working on his first batch of homebrew. He wasn't ready to go into the beer business.

Even though he didn't begin his career in the beer industry right there, this moment did wake up the entrepreneurial spirit which Ron would utilize from that point forward. With no prospect of owning his own brewery in the short term, Ron turned his energy to working with a mentoring professor at the University of Michigan to let him focus his Masters work on brewing.

While they didn't have a program, through a collaboration with his sponsoring professor, he was able to work out a curriculum which was approved by the University. Years later he would be relaying that very story on a tour at his business. The Dean of the School of Natural Resources from the University of Michigan happened to be on it. He quickly informed Ron that under the charters and rules currently governing the University he would not be allowed to create his own curriculum.

Lucky for him it wasn't the case at the time!

After graduation he went to work for a company in Michigan which owned and operated brewpubs. He became involved in not only brewing, but specialized in opening new stores. The money wasn't great; in fact, he had to work two other jobs just to make ends meet. More important than pay was the fact he was learning on the job. What he was getting out of this experience was knowledge of every facet of running a brewery and a brewpub.

After nine years, he felt confident in his ability to run his own business. One day, as he was sitting on the porch enjoying an imported sour style beer, he said to his wife Laurie, "If I could just make beer like this for a living, wouldn't that be awesome?" They began to work on a plan for a craft brewery.

The name Jolly Pumpkin came out of a process of simply coming up with a long list of names. As they kept refining and revising the list, the name Jolly Pumpkin stood out. It was almost like Ron couldn't say the name with a straight face. Since he was looking to do something he wanted to have fun with, it seemed like a perfect fit.

With interest in craft brewing picking up rapidly, Ron needed something to stand out from the competition. His idea was to focus on oak-aged sour beers, like the ones he and Laurie had been enjoying on their porch the day they decided to start their brewery. This process involves aging ingredients in oak barrels using only the wild yeasts, i.e. the naturally occurring yeasts in the barrel. The mixture ferments with notes of tropical with hints of leather and tobacco coming from the oak. The product ends up with a lighter body and is higher in carbonation than most beers. Almost like a champagne.

This is a process almost as old as brewing itself. In fact, they had a name for what we now call oak-aged sour beer. It was simply called, "beer." Prior to the fancy equipment, and specialized yeast strands of today, fermenting ingredients in barrels was the way beer was made. Consistency is gained through blending which is exactly what Ron Jeffries does today.

Since there was such a sense of artistry to the crafting of his oak-aged sour beers, Ron added Artisan Ales to make the company officially Jolly Pumpkin Artisan Ales. After securing funding through a local bank, Ron got to work on a shoestring budget. He bought used equipment and did the installation himself.

Standing out in a growing market is certainly an enviable position. You don't want to stand too far from the crowd, though. It's almost what happened to Ron with his line of oak-aged sour beers.

Being so different than anything on the market meant there really wasn't a demand for it. Since he didn't have the marketing budget of a megabrand, it was challenging to educate consumers so they would try it.

Luckily for Ron, there were a few people who did get it. He even made a bit of a splash at the Great American Beer Festival his first year. As consumers became more and more interested in craft beers, their sense of adventurism led them to try more new beers. Soon, oak-aged sour beers were on the radar of American beer drinkers. More competitors joined him with their own offerings of oak-aged sour beers. He welcomed the competition since he had been at the forefront of a new segment and needed more offerings to increase interest and demand from consumers.

As business began to grow, Ron and Laurie began wondering how to take their business to the next stage of growth. About this same time, he had some potential investors approach him with an interesting proposition. They wanted to invest in his business and in-turn have him help open some brewpubs with them. With his background, he was perfect for this job. Plus, this could only help grow his Jolly Pumpkin business.

Knowing he was going to diversify his business, he started a new umbrella company, Northern United Brewing Company which would be the parent for all of these businesses.

Today, he runs two brewpubs, a brewery and a winery. The next phase is even bolder. He and Laurie love to vacation in Hawai'i. They envision a brewpub there where they could produce a unique line of beers using local ingredients. In addition to the brewery, Ron really wants to pursue another passion and open a longboard skateboard and surfboard shop. What better marrying of hobbies could there be than beer, food, surfing and skateboarding, all with the backdrop of Hawai'i?

If, or when, that happens is still to be determined. As you can imagine Ron stays pretty busy with the businesses he is currently running. Not only does he continue to brew when he can, he stays actively engaged in the operations of all of his businesses.

One area he has been focusing on recently is partnerships where two breweries work together to release a beer. He had done this in the past but had been so busy growing his business, he hadn't done one in awhile. A project last fall put him in touch with a friend in the industry, and they had a collaboration which went well, leading him to seek out more.

Another highlight in running his business is the fact Ron gets to work with his family. Don't forget, he's the guy who once quit a band so he could focus on family. Today he not only works with wife Laurie, but his son Daemon has joined the business as well.

Whether or not Ron and Laurie end up in Hawai'i, it is readily apparent that they have plenty to be jolly about!
e

Jolly Pumpkin Artisan Ales Photo Album

Ron and Laurie Jeffries

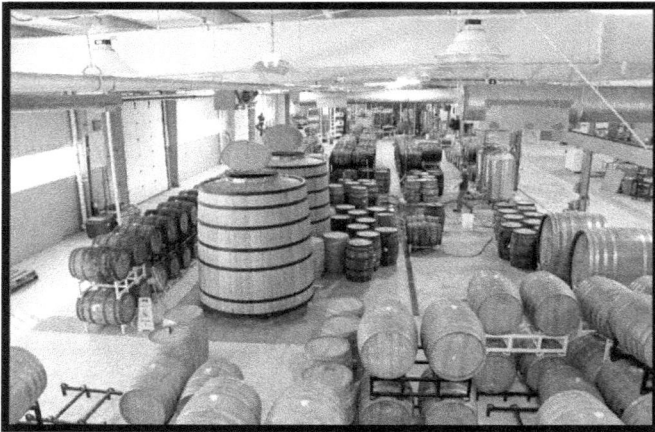

Barrels of beer at the warehouse

Ron in front of some of his foudres (aging casks)

Ron with some of his medals

Jolly Pumpkin product lineup

Chapter 15
Lakefront Brewery, Inc.

1872 N. Commerce Street
Milwaukee, WI 53212
(414) 372-8800

lakefrontbrewery.com
info@lakefrontbrewery.com

Established
1987

Leadership
Russ Klisch, Founder, Owner and President
Jim Klisch, Founder, Sales and Marketing

"Our first batch of homebrew came with the usual assessment of anyone's first crack at making beer; we were excited because it wasn't that bad."
   -Jim Klisch

In the mid-80s, Russ Klisch was a chemical engineer, and his brother Jim was a Milwaukee policeman. One day, the brothers, who were living together, decided to have a beer after work. Then something happened which would change their entire career paths and lead to the formation of Lakefront Brewery.

It seemed so simple.

Jim, who was enjoying his frosty one, asked Russ, "How do you make beer?"

It seemed like a logical question. After all, Russ was a chemical engineer. Certainly, he would know how to make something as common as beer. They probably even teach beer making at some point in college, right?

Nope.

Russ had no idea how to make beer. He was more in tune with the drinking side of beer than the production side. The brothers had a good laugh and did some further research into the "drinking side of beer" that night.

As far as Jim was concerned, the whole episode was over the night it happened. Apparently, it stuck with Russ, though. Two weeks later, on Jim's birthday, Russ gave him a book about making beer as a gift.

The brothers once again had a good laugh and rehashed their night of drinking a few weeks before. Now, it was Russ' turn to think the whole situation was case closed. He had given Jim the prank gift and, in reality, didn't think Jim would actually read it.

Not only did Jim read it, he was inspired to try his hand at making beer. To the surprise of the brothers, it really wasn't that bad. Soon, Russ decided he needed to give beer making a try, too.

Before long, the brothers were making some really great beers. Friends and family encouraged their efforts, so they began entering their beers in contests. Just like the feedback they had gotten from the people they knew, the judges of the contest, also liked what the Klisch brothers were doing.

With the awards piling up and a desire to try something new, the brothers decided to move forward with opening a brewery. They got lucky and were able to secure the site for their business. The bought a building which once housed an old bakery. The best part was the fact the building not only had a perfect place for the production area (sloped floors and utility feeds) where they would be able to brew but four apartments had been added. Russ and Jim had a major build-out on the brewery side and were able to utilize the cash flow from the renters to assist in running their fledgling business. This would be an important component to their early success as Russ and Jim weren't able to get any financing. Everything came out-of-pocket so a monthly income would be vital to keeping things going.

While Russ' engineering background might not have been helpful in knowing how beer was brewed when Jim first asked, it was another key component for the brothers building their brewery. They would literally buy tanks at scrap prices, and then Russ would go all "MacGyver" and turn them into working tanks for the brewery.

During their education for opening a brewery, Russ attended a seminar where the topic of naming a brewery came up. The individual leading the class suggested that naming a brewery a family name or after a city was passé. Russ, inspired by the meeting, began thinking about what name might convey Milwaukee without actually using it in the name. He came up with Lakefront. He thought it would convey the good times people have when they are enjoying themselves on a lake vacation or at a family lake home. He also thought it was a natural tie-in to the city of Milwaukee with Lake Michigan so associated with the town.

The only problem was the fact the brewery wasn't on Lake Michigan or any other body of water, either. It would cause much confusion over the years although the move of the brewery in 1998 would put them on the Milwaukee River so at least they are on a body of water now... even if it is a river instead of a lake.

Initially, they were only kegging their beer, literally, for a single customer. After a time of only selling beer to their one customer, business did begin to pick up. They started adding more accounts one at a time through the efforts of the brothers, all done in their spare time (at first, they continued to work their full-time jobs while working at the brewery in the evenings, on weekends and on vacation days from their jobs).

Eventually, they would begin bottling. Just like he had with the entire brewery, when they decided to start bottling, Russ built his own bottler. Like the brewery, he made it out of scrap and spare parts. In fact, they gave it the name Gizmo since it seemed to have its own personality. It only filled a single bottle at a time which then needed to be hand-labeled and packed, but it was a baby step towards taking their business to the next level.

The initial beer recipes, one from each brother, are still produced today, and they remain some of their most popular offerings. Riverwest Stein is an amber lager created by Jim and is their number one selling beer. Klisch Pilsner is the beer Russ formulated, and it is a traditional European pilsner.

Visiting Lakefront Brewery may be an experience like no other craft brewery. According to online rating site Trip Advisor, Lakefront is the top-rated brewery tour in Milwaukee. That fact alone is saying something. Let's not forget, Milwaukee is known as a beer town. It has some of the largest, most well-known breweries in the country located there. Standing out above them is clearly an indicator the lengths Lakefront goes to provide an experience for its visitors.

This is accomplished by hiring the right types of individuals first and foremost. Lakefront hires improv artists, comedians and actors. These are people who know how to interact with people, are able to make things fun and are certainly used to working in front of an audience.

The company's dedication doesn't stop there. These aren't just displaced showbiz types. They actually are put to work learning all facets of the brewery as well as the industry. This all comes together to provide an informative, fun and interactive tour (hint: there may be a sing-along and recreation of the Laverne and Shirley theme song complete with a glove traveling down the bottling line).

As if that wasn't enough, Russ and Jim have taken the experience of visiting Lakefront Brewing a step further by bringing some uniquely Milwaukee items to the tours. In County Stadium, the old ballpark of the Milwaukee Brewers, the mascot had an area where he would go down a slide and into a mug of beer when things got exciting in a Brewers' game. It was known as the Brewer's Chalet. When the team moved into their new stadium, they announced they were selling the chalet, and the Klisches bought it. Baseball fans love to get their photos taken by this unique piece of Brewers' history.

The Klisches also picked up some historic lights from a hotel which broke ground in 1916. They hung in the banquet room until the hotel was demolished in 1982, and then sat in a city-owned warehouse. The lights were worthy of historic preservation as they represented an important piece of Milwaukee architectural history since were crafted in a combination art nouveau/arts and crafts style.

When the city of Milwaukee announced they were selling them with a starting bid of $5,000, the Klisch brothers bid $5,013. Even though a Chicago bidder placed a $10,000 bid, the city accepted the Klisch brothers' bid since they would not only be kept in Milwaukee, they would be displayed to the public.

For the Klisch brothers, it's pretty powerful to see the impact their 150 employee company now has on the local economy and the families of its employees. It amazing for them to think about how all of this got started with a simple question about how to brew beer.

Currently, Lakefront is in the process of adding space to the warehouse and new equipment. Having just surpassed 44,000 barrels of beer recently, the company is growing quickly. Though it has taken them over 25 years to get there, the Klisch brothers see 100,000 barrels in the not so distant future. They are on pace to go from a regional to national brewer in short order.

Future growth will likely mean the need for another plant. Who knows, it may even be lakefront property!

Lakefront Brewery Photo Album

Jim and Russ Klisch

1987 article announcing their first barrels being produced

The original brewery

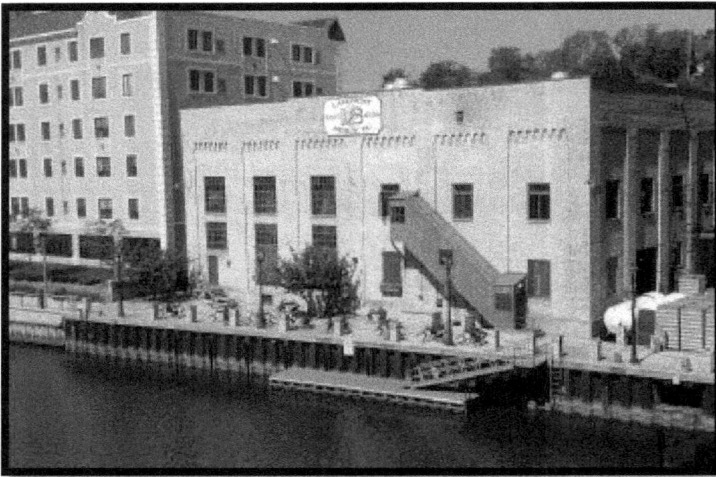

The new brewery (on the Milwaukee River)

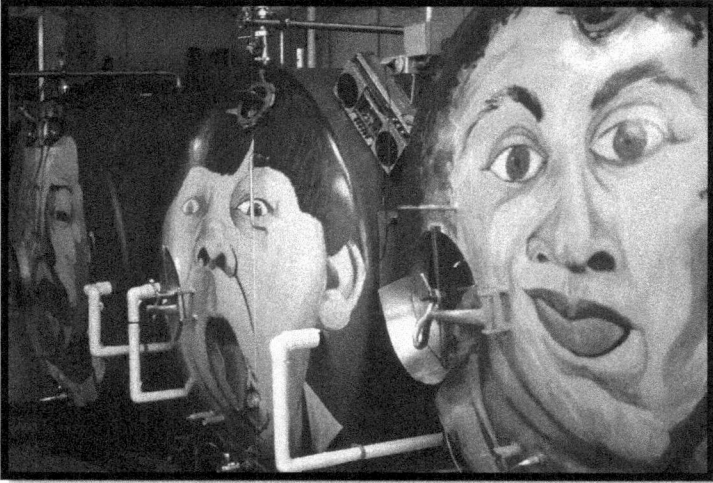

Russ' "Frankenstein" tank system dressed up with paintings of the Three Stooges

Delivery van

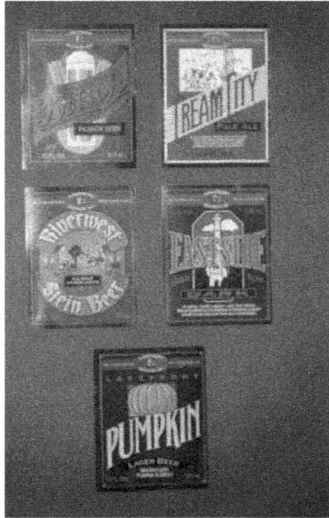

A look at some of the labels from the archives

Lakefront Brewery product lineup

Chapter 16
Lazy Magnolia Brewing Company

7030 Roscoe-Turner Road
Kiln, MS 39556
(228) 467-2727

lazymagnolia.com
info@lazymagnolia.com

Established
2003

Leadership
Mark and Leslie Henderson, Co-Owners and General Managers

"Even more than opening a business, we wanted to bring an industry to the State of Mississippi."
      -Leslie Henderson

An electrical engineer and a chemical engineer walk into a bar...

For most, that statement sounds like the start of a bad joke. At Lazy Magnolia Brewing Company, though, it sounds like a sales call.

Mississippi natives Mark and Leslie Henderson met at Mississippi State University. Both were studying engineering. Mark was in the electrical engineering program, and Leslie was studying to be a chemical engineer.

The two began dating while at MSU and, ultimately, would get married. Upon graduating college, both began working in the fields they had studied. Mark secured a job at an electrical engineer firm working on RADAR systems. Leslie went to work in chemical engineering at a small plastics plant.

Mark and Leslie each looked at their jobs as a stopgap. In the long-term, they didn't want to work for someone else. The key was to find something which appealed to both of them equally since they wanted a business where they could work together.

As they began vetting out potential businesses to start, they decided to take a look at Mark's hobby. Mark had been a homebrewer and always received rave reviews for the beer he made. Conversations about starting a brewery would often arise from those who tasted his beer.

On the positive side, the business appealed to both of them. Mark's background as a homebrewer and his ability to handle the build out/running of the equipment with his electrical engineering background made him a perfect candidate to be in the business. Leslie really enjoyed brewing as well. She loved the science behind the combining of ingredients and natural occurrences which happen during the brewing process.

On the negative side, craft brewing hadn't yet come to Mississippi. The south, in general, was behind the whole craft brewing movement, but Mississippi lagged behind its surrounding states.

The laws were prohibitive for running a craft brewery, and there wasn't a built-in demand like other areas where craft brewing was established, but still, Mark and Leslie wanted to give the notion of opening a brewery its due diligence.

As they began researching the potential of a craft brewery, they assessed that while challenging, it could be done. What really sold them on the idea was their excitement transcended simply doing something they both enjoyed. It became about bringing a new industry to the State of Mississippi.

They knew that if they were successful, they could assist in changing the laws and help with starting a new industry. The potential to create jobs as well as make customers happy with their product was enough for Mark and Leslie to start their business.

The challenges of starting a brewery in Mississippi did go beyond the laws surrounding selling beer. The logistics of brewing in a large scale commercial operation was an issue. There wasn't a supplier of the raw ingredients in nearby states, so Mark and Leslie spent a lot of time traveling to assemble ingredients.

Without any competitors, Mark and Leslie were also taking a leap of faith that consumers would acquire a taste for craft beers. Even though Mark had always gotten accolades for the homebrews he created, there was some worry as to whether or not they would be able to build the client base needed to support a craft brewery since the beers they were creating would be very different from the light beers associated with the big American brewers.

The mantra they established between them to overcome the hesitancy surrounding the questions about whether or not they would find an audience for their beer came from a quote from Steve Jobs. Steve had once stated, "People don't know what they want until you show it to them." Mark and Leslie knew that if they were able to get customers to try their beer, the demand for it would follow.

One piece of business in getting started that was easy was the name: Lazy Magnolia Brewing Company. Everything Mark and Leslie were all about pointed back to it as being the perfect name. First and foremost is the fact Mississippi is known as "The Magnolia State. Secondly, the moniker "Lazy Magnolia" conveyed a sense of laid back conversations amongst friends enjoying beer. It seemed like the perfect message to promote their brand.

There is also the need to select a name which is easy to remember and just rolls off the tongue: "I'll take a Lazy Magnolia."

Check!

Finally, the real item that sealed the deal making Lazy Magnolia the company name was the personal connection Mark and Leslie had to it. They have a magnolia tree which shades their back porch. It's on that porch where Mark would do all of his homebrewing.

The Lazy Magnolia Brewing Company: perfection!

Today, Mark and Leslie have a brand which is doing exactly what they envisioned when they started the company over 11 years ago. They are currently available in 14 states and have additional states in the works to expand their distribution even further. While state laws do not allow them to self-distribute their product, they work closely with the sales reps from their distributors, training them on their product as well as introducing them to opportunities. (Yes, there really are times when an electrical engineer and a chemical engineer are walking into a bar...)

Their most popular beer is their Southern Pecan which highlights their position as a southern craft brewer. According to Lazy Magnolia's website, it is the first beer made of roasted pecans and is a lightly hopped beer offering a nutty, caramel, malty taste throughout its complex flavor profile.

They are in a facility with a capacity up to 50,000 barrels, so they have plenty of room to continue to grow and expand. They offer tours on Thursdays, Fridays and Saturdays from dedicated tour guides who make the tours educational and fun.

Individuals taking the tours get to enjoy samples of six different beers while they are there. Lazy Magnolia doesn't have a taproom where individuals can buy a pint... at least not yet. Mark and Leslie have remained active in working on legislation to make the State of Mississippi more appealing to craft brewers, and while they have made great strides from where they were when they began, they still have work to do. Their next big project is to get the law changed which forbids them from offering the sale of pints which would certainly enhance the visitor experience of their facility.

Mark and Leslie forecast continued growth for their company over the next five years. Let's not forget this is an electrical and chemical engineer providing this forecasting. It's a pretty safe bet they are going to be right on with their numbers!

Still, for all of the success they have achieved, getting to this point what remains the most satisfying for Mark and Leslie is the positive impact they are having on their home state of Mississippi. Their work not only creates jobs at their brewery, it has created jobs across the state as more breweries have continued to pop up.

Leslie sums it up best when she says, "Our mission is to make the State of Mississippi better one pint at a time."

Lazy Magnolia Brewing Company Photo Album

Leslie and Mark Henderson

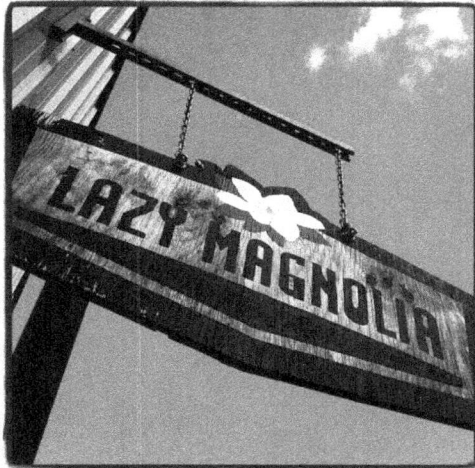

Outside the Lazy Magnolia brewery

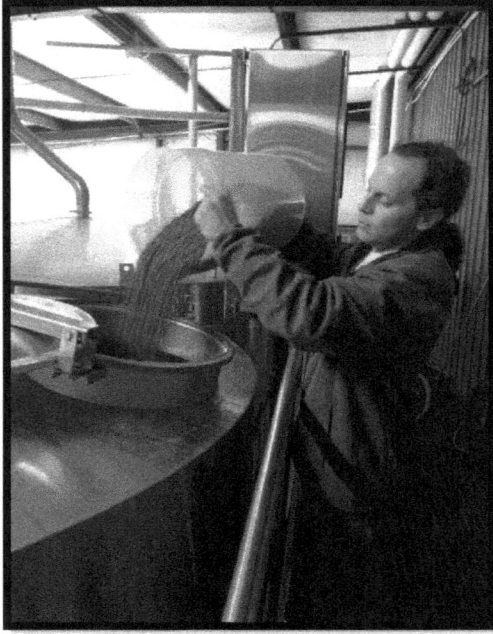

It's time to make the beer

Kegged and ready to go

Working an event

Racked

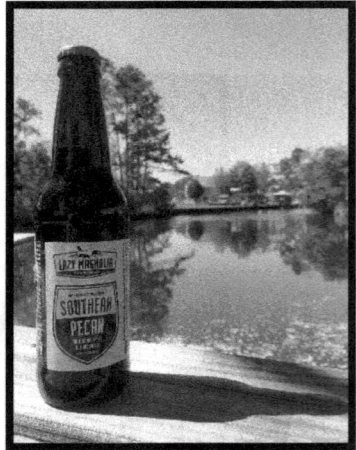

Lazy Magnolia product lineup

Chapter 17
Lucid Brewing

6020 Culligan Way
Minnetonka, MN 55345
(612) 615-8243

lucidbrewing.com

Established
2011

Leadership
Eric Biermann, President and Head Brewer
Jon Messier, Vice President

"We had our lucid moment when we were drinking beers and talking about quitting our corporate jobs."
-Jon Messier

The basic recipe for beer involves hops, barley, yeast and water. Mix together and wait.

The recipe for starting a brewery involves a couple of avid homebrewers, some office jobs and a few cubicles. Mix together and wait.

Minnesota residents Eric Biermann and Jon Messier may not be following the basic recipe for beer when they are creating the outstanding and unique beers their company produces, but they definitely followed the basic recipe to start their business.

Jon was an aerospace engineer. Over the years, he worked a couple of corporate jobs. First, he was testing structures and weapons, and then he moved into quality assurance. The funny thing was, the more "successful" he became in his career, with promotions and advancements in the companies he worked for, the worse his jobs got. Each step up, meant less time doing fun aerospace engineering duties and more time in a suit and tie delivering PowerPoint presentations.

It wasn't much different for Eric Biermann. He was an international accountant for a multi-national organization. He spent his days tethered to a desk crunching numbers.

Days in the rack of a corporate gig means you can use a hobby; something to expand the mind and provide a creative outlet. For both Jon and Eric, their stress-relieving hobby was brewing beer. In fact, they took their hobby pretty seriously. As such, they were not only members of the local beer club, they were actively engaged in the running of the organization.

This wasn't any ordinary beer club with a once a year meeting and a "quarterly newsletter" which comes out once or twice a year. They met monthly and about 50 – 60 people attended every meeting. Attendees would bring their most recent brews and some food. These would literally turn into pot-luck style dinners with individuals tasting each other's offerings and providing critical feedback. It was always amazing to see the more experienced individuals who would be able to see where a beer had gone wrong in the brewing process simply by tasting it.

For most, that would be the end of the story. Corporate job by day, brewing hobby at night. At this point, Jon and Eric starting a brewery together could not be foreseen. They really couldn't be classified as anything other than acquaintances. They only knew each other from the club and did not get together socially outside of club events.

From spending some time with Eric at club functions, Jon did know that Eric was looking ahead to life beyond the corporate world. He had started taking some classes which he thought would help him in either working for a brewery, or perhaps starting his own operation. That little nugget of information stuck in Jon's mind when a friend of a friend, who knew Jon did some brewing, suggested he buy a building he owned as he thought it would be perfect for a brewery.

Jon wasn't interested in trying to tackle the job of handling a start-up on his own, so he reached out to Eric. Jon was pleased to find Eric was open to the idea of working with him, so they checked out the building. Despite the fact the building needed a lot of work, they saw the vision of the facility and the location, so they made the move and purchased it.

Luckily for the duo, both Jon and Eric had professional wives with the demeanors of saints, so they were able to leave their jobs and work full-time on their new brewery. There was plenty of work to be done. In addition to the cumbersome build-out, they had the local, state and federal paperwork to fill out and get approved.

The first step to starting a business is always securing the name. Defined, lucid means, "clarity in thinking or vision." Both Jon and Eric liked the idea of using it as the name of the company. It tied back to their own personal stories (the clarity to recognize the dead-end corporate world and take a chance on working for themselves) and they liked the saying, "From clarity in thinking comes excellence in drinking." It's the mission statement, rally cry and marching orders for the company all wrapped up into one word: lucid.

Lucid Brewery became the name of their business.

In addition to a name, Jon and Eric knew the look of their business would be the key. In order to figure out exactly what they wanted for their logos and labeling, they went on an art history tour. They knew they wanted a bold look and not something passive. They also decided they would not have any dogs, mountains, streams or prairies involved in their branding. All of those entities seemed a little played out to them.

The concept of an "art history tour" for a couple of guys starting a brewery seems a little farfetched. Perhaps they were taking advantage of their hardworking wives who were now each keeping their respective homes together on single incomes. In reality, it worked out perfectly. Jon and Eric discovered a sect of art known as "The Futurists." This movement was big in Italy in the 1920s and featured sharp edges, color layering and industrial components.

Not only were they fans of the style, the tie-in to their own fondness for art, combined with the fact it draws from an industrial look, was perfect. After all, their building had an industrial/warehouse-type feel to it.

Employing the approach of The Futurists, Eric and Jon commissioned the design of their logo which ended up featuring a single eye. It gives the company a look which carries throughout all of its products.

In order to upgrade the equipment they had planned to purchase, Eric and Jon turned to the website Kickstarter. On the site, individuals are allowed to invest in a project without taking an equity stake in the business. Instead of giving away a percentage of business, for these small investments they are typically given a small token gift, like a t-shirt. Eric and Jon had a successful campaign where they were able to raise the $10,000 they needed.

It meant a lot for Jon and Eric to give a chance for their old buddies in the brewing club to assist them in starting their business with small, affordable contributions. They have also found the individuals who participated in their Kickstarter campaign have remained loyal patrons and often interact with Jon and Eric at events.

Initially, the twosome started delivering the beer they created themselves. They found it difficult to grow their business while keeping their current customers happy. Soon, they decided to go through distributors, employing their own sales team to serve as a liaison between the company and the distributors as well as the restaurants, bars, grocery and liquor stores they sell to. This has proven to be a successful model and really helped the brand take off.

Currently, Lucid is available throughout Minnesota along with parts of North and South Dakota. Further distribution into all three of those states, along with entrance into Iowa and Wisconsin is planned for this year. Jon and Eric expect this growth to continue in upcoming years and anticipate Lucid to be a regional brand.

Certainly, there are challenges to running a small company and taking a new brand to market. With these challenges, though, come many rewards. Jon and Eric get to experience firsthand the excitement and enthusiasm of people who enjoy the product they create.

Plus, it's just fun. Jon and Eric are passionate about discovering solutions to the challenges of finding ways to beat the big guys.

Best of all… they don't have to wear ties anymore!

Lucid Brewing Photo Album

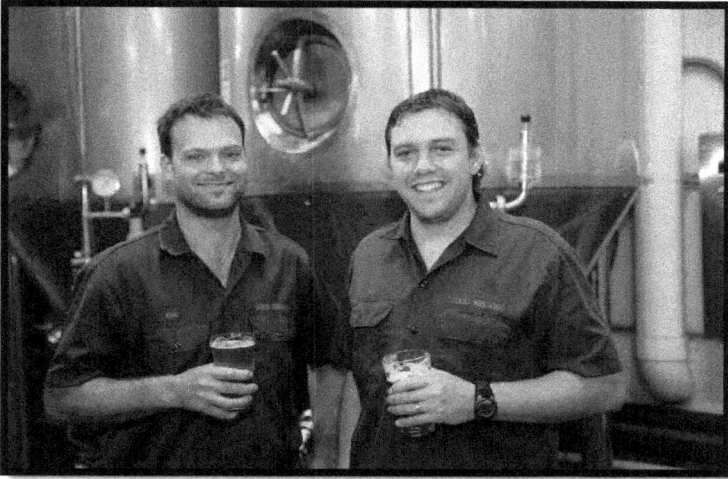

Eric Biermann and Jon Messier

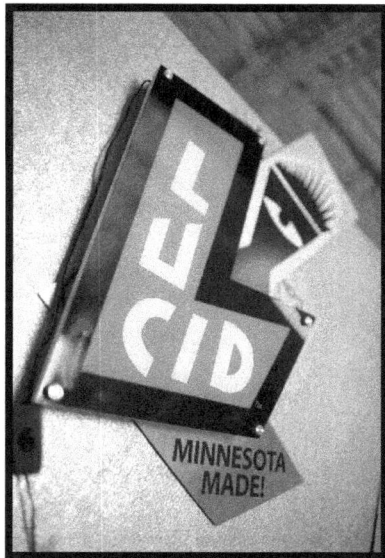

Sign at the Lucid Brewing brewery

Bottles of beer

Kegs of beer

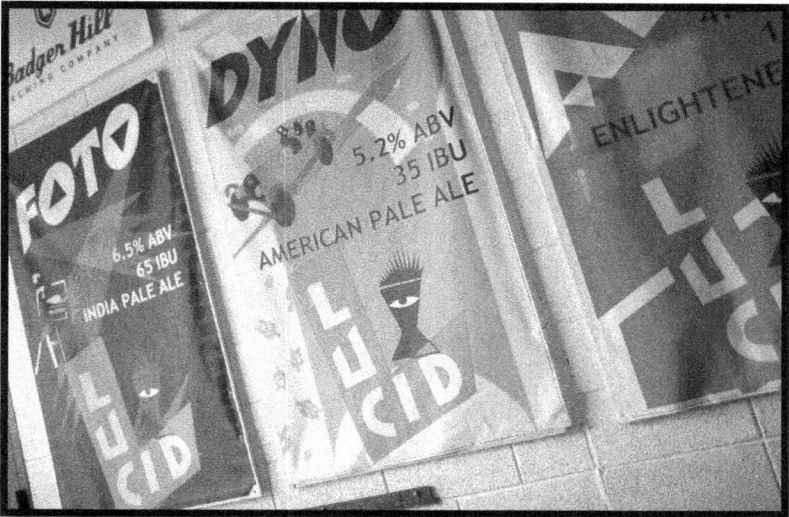

Wouldn't you like to see the size of the bottle these labels fit?

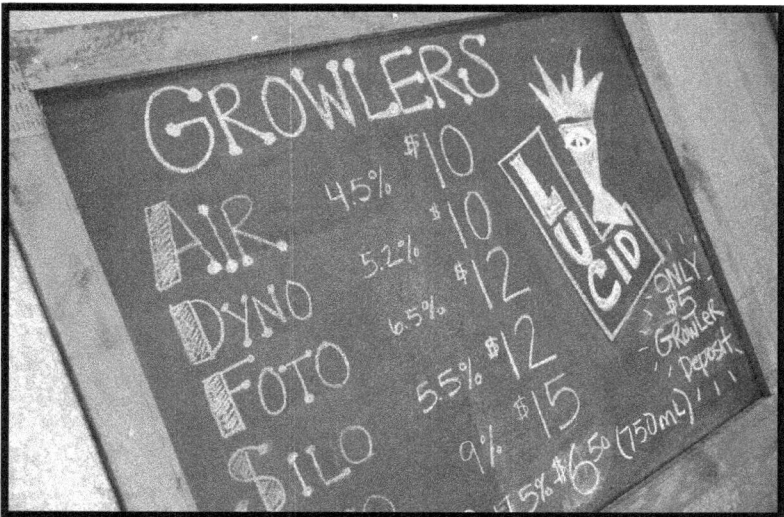

Selling good beer… and good cheer!

Lucid Brewing packaging detail

Lucid Brewing product lineup

Chapter 18
Mad River Brewing Company

195 Taylor Way
Blue Lake, CA 95525
(707) 669-4151

madriverbrewing.com
website@madriverbrewing.com

Established
1989

Leadership
Bob Smith, Founder
Charlie Jordan, CEO
Dylan Schatz, Brew Master

"I have an appreciation for people who have a passion for what they do."
      -Charlie Jordan

Long before it was trendy to brew beer in your house, Humboldt County, California, resident Bob Smith was taking homebrewing to the extreme. He immersed himself in learning as much as he could about his hobby. His dream of the end goal was being able to turn his passion for crafting beer into a way to make a living by opening his own brewery. With the lack of information available at the time, Bob Smith founded the "Humbrewers Guild," which fostered an environment of sharing both product samples for critical feedback, best practices and information for brewers in and around Humboldt County.

Bob's hobby also brought him to the homebrew shop of Ken Grossman in Chico, California. The two struck up a friendship over their shared desire to open a brewery. In 1979, Ken's dream turned into reality when he started Sierra Nevada Brewing Company (yes, it's that Sierra Nevada). The two remained friends, and Bob got to witness firsthand the transition from a hobby brewery to a business. Bob was inspired to take action on starting his own company as Sierra Nevada realized some early success.

In 1989, Bob Smith opened the Mad River Brewing Company in Blue Lake, California (Humboldt County, of course), about 60 yards from the Mad River. The Mad River is revered by fisherman for its steelhead runs. Not only did Mad River inspire the name of the company, it inspired Steelhead Ale which would become the brewery's flagship beer line. (Mad River's Steelhead Extra Pale Ale is their most popular beer today.)

Bob's old friend Ken Grossman also proved to be an invaluable contact in helping Bob during those early years.

As Sierra Nevada had a decade head start on Mad River, Bob was able to buy some of the equipment Sierra Nevada had outgrown. The company's first seventeen barrel brewing system and bottling line came from Sierra Nevada.

In order to continue to offer a quality product, Bob was steadfast in his desire to remain a small local brewer. Fans of his beer felt differently. Demand meant the company continued to grow even as Bob envisioned staying with the microbrewer approach.

As the company continued to find success, Bob took a bit of a step back from the business. He trained new brewers and hired a management team to handle the day-to-day operations of his growing business.

One of the individuals hired during this time was Dylan Schatz. Dylan had been in the construction industry but the owner of the company he worked for decided to take some time off from the business, so he was left unemployed. Though he had no experience working in the beer industry, he did like the idea of the artistry of brewing since he was a passionate home chef who enjoyed pairing ingredients in his cooking. He applied for a position at Mad River and was pleased to get hired.

Of course, there wasn't much artistry in Dylan's first job in the beer industry. He started his career working on the bottling line with another employee. Three days into his job, the other employee quit, and Dylan was left to run the bottling line by himself.

Hey, three days in, and he was already promoted!

Over the next several years, Dylan would work in many other areas of the company until he finally landed where he truly wanted to be: in brewing. It was there he would finally be able to apply some of the skills in the area of flavor profiles he had acquired in the kitchen to making beer. Dylan would eventually work his way up to becoming the company's Brew Master.

Over time, company founder Bob Smith began to look towards retirement. Additionally, the managing director he had hired was also looking ahead towards retirement, so the company began actively looking for someone new to run the organization.

Around this time, Charlie Jordan was also looking for a new opportunity. She had spent the first 25 years of her career in product development in hard goods working on the mechanical/production side. The last several years leading up to this point, she had transitioned to consumer goods and had worked with several food and beverage companies. Her area of specialty was leading turnarounds for organizations which were struggling.

When she interviewed with Mad River Brewing Company, she found a situation with a great infrastructure. They offered a quality product and had an excellent team in place. The biggest issues they seemed to be facing was the fact they were seemingly at capacity in their current location, and they needed assistance on the sales side.

After going through the interview process, Mad River extended Charlie an offer, and she accepted, joining the company as its CEO. One of her first jobs was to look at production. With the company running at full capacity, increasing revenue would be difficult if they didn't have the opportunity to gain market share by brewing more beer.

Charlie notes that one of her biggest challenges in starting with the organization was simply to get individuals to think differently. She states that making changes to the processes individuals are used to can be even more challenging than simply starting with a new company, which would have a clean slate. By implementing some changes in procedures, and taking a fresh look at production, they were able to significantly increase capacity without being forced into making large capital investments in new equipment.

Under Charlie's leadership, and Dylan's creativity, the Mad River team looks to continue to grow the business. Recently, the company finally exceeded 15,000 barrels a year in production which officially moved them from a small brewer to a regional brewer. Today, they are producing 18,000 barrels a year, going to 22,000 barrels next year with plans to increase production to about 100,000 in the next 5 – 8 years.

When they reach this goal, they will be looking at a whole new era in the company's history as they will need to look at another brewery to increase production beyond there. Whether that is a completely new facility, or a second site, remains to be seen.

Truth be told, the Mad River team isn't looking that far ahead. One mistake Charlie and Dylan do not want to make is a common one they have seen from many of their fellow craft brewers as they began to expand: quality starts to slip. The only way Charlie and Dylan can envision their organization continuing to extend its reach is if they are able to oversee the production, growth, and distribution, in a manner allowing them to offer the same quality their customers have come to know and expect.

Mad River beers are currently available in 28 states. The company continues to be an active part of the community in Humboldt County, participating in numerous festivals and events.

Dylan Schatz has realized the ultimate dream for himself in that not only is he creating respected and unique beers, he also gets to put his love of cooking to use, as well. One of the company's most popular events are their Brew Master dinners which features menus and beers paired together, with major input from Dylan.

Today, the brewery is open seven days a week. A visit to Mad River offers unique experiences in tours, tastings and a kitchen which offers a menu built using good quality ingredients such as grass fed beef, high quality sustainable fish and organic produce. Best of all, visitors get to interact with the staff and see the passion every employee brings to their jobs at Mad River Brewing.

Under the guidance of the "other dynamic duo" of Charlie Jordan and Dylan Schatz, it's hard to imagine they won't reach their ultimate capacity of 100,000 barrels at their current location at the nearer edge of their 5 – 8 year projection. No matter when it happens, two things are certain:

1). They will be well positioned for the growth under the leadership of Charlie and Dylan.

2). The beer from their 100,000th barrel will taste just as good as the beer from their 1st.

Charlie and Dylan wouldn't have it any other way.

Mad River Brewing Company Photo Album

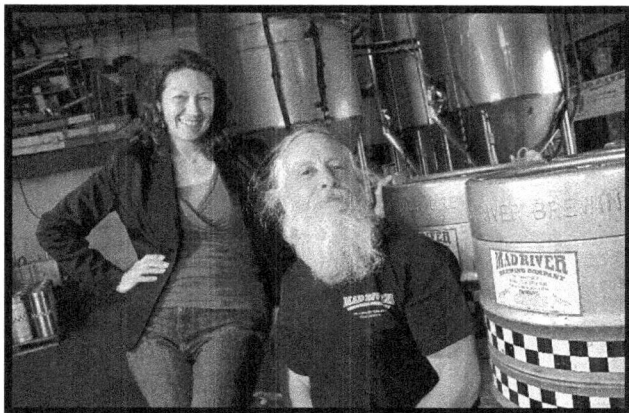

Charlie Jordan and Bob Smith

Dylan Schatz

Bob Smith (left) at the brewery ribbon cutting in 1989

The Mad River team celebrating a silver at the Great
American Beer Festival

Serving up some pints in the taproom

Fun out in the beer garden

The Mad River production crew

Mad River product lineup

Chapter 19
Mother's Brewing Company

215 South Grant
Springfield, MO 65806
(417) 862-0423

mothersbrewing.com
info@mothersbrewing.com

Established
2011

Leadership
Jeff Schrag, Founder

"Craft beer combines the traditions of the beer world with the artistry of the wine world."
-Jeff Schrag

Jeff Schrag grew up in Central Kansas. He attended Kansas State University where he studied journalism. Rather than working in the media, he decided to put his degree to work in a different way: he bought a small weekly newspaper.

While it wasn't the path to riches, it was just successful enough to allow him to buy another newspaper. He continued doing this and before long he was adding other companies outside of the newspaper industry to his portfolio as well.

Buying and selling businesses, Jeff became the epitome of the serial entrepreneur. One common bond of the serial entrepreneur set is that they love to gamble. Jeff had gambled his safety net of financial security many times throughout the course of his career. Whether he was good, lucky, an expert of timing, or simply a combination of all of the above, he certainly had more winners than losers in his track record.

Utilizing the approach of having three simple guiding principles to success has proven to be key for Jeff in running his businesses:

1. Write down what you believe in and what you want to accomplish.

2. Detail how you are going to accomplish your plan.

3. Refer back to your written plan frequently to make sure you are following your plan exactly as you wrote it.

In 2008, Jeff wanted to test his approach and his luck one more time. He felt like there was one last roll of the dice for him. It would require him to gamble everything, though, to do it right. He wanted to open up a brewery.

The thought of a craft brewery felt right to him. Being a good steward of the community and a place where people could meet was something he had always dreamed about.

Jeff was also a person who believed in the concept of the American downtown. Being able to open a business in the heart of the community would be a key component to completing his vision. He simply loved the idea of being able to brew the best beer in the world right in his current hometown of Springfield, Missouri.

While he wasn't a home brewer, like so many who get started in craft brewing, he does note he is an enthusiastic drinker. He even had a bit of history in trying to get into the beer business. As a young man he saw the Kansas Wheat Commission was offering grants for individuals starting businesses utilizing Kansas wheat. He pitched the idea of a Kansas wheat beer but was turned down.

In preparation for opening his business, he went to work studying the industry. He joined the Brewer's Association which offered him resources and guidance for getting started. He also supplemented his knowledge by reading books and visiting breweries where he would engage the owners in conversation about his plans. He found them to be very forthcoming in the advice they gave him.

The greatest challenge he had was securing capital. By the time he was moving to implement his plan, the economy was starting to recover but banks were still reluctant to invest in a business like the one he was proposing.

Ultimately, he was able to find a bank which was open to his ideas and saw his vision. Being that he wasn't a brewer himself, his first order of business was to hire a brewmaster to help him out. For that, he turned to *match.com*.

Seriously.

Okay, admittedly, it's probably not like you are thinking. He didn't put a profile up stating "*Man Seeking Brewmaster*," though that's not a bad idea. A woman he met on the online dating website introduced him to Brian Allen. Brian had 15 years brewing experience but had recently moved to Springfield for his wife's job (she had just received her Ph.D. and had just secured a professorship at a university in town). With their move, Brian was out of work. Jeff was able to hire him, and the two began to lay out the plans for their business.

They got lucky when the building which had been the site of an old bakery became available. Not only were they in downtown Springfield, the location had plenty of room for production, a tasting room and tours. They had plenty of room to expand before they would ever need to look elsewhere for space. Their location would allow them to produce approximately 50,000 barrels a year, which under current production numbers, would put them in the top 75 craft brewers in the United States.

Despite the popularity of brewpubs, Jeff wanted to be sure to keep his company a production-only brewery. He knew that if he opened a restaurant, he would be competing directly with the bars and restaurants he would be trying to sell beer to, and he felt it wasn't good for business.

Jeff's other good fortune in starting his business came through the hiring of Jeremy Wicker. Jeremy, a branding and marketing expert who was looking to move home to Springfield, was the final cog to help make Mother's Brewing Company a success. His expertise in positioning and marketing their product was a key area of knowledge Jeff would need for his first foray into a consumer packaged product.

Their idea for success was to swim in two streams. They would offer "introductory" beers for the person new to craft brewing. As Jeff states, these are, "honest beers," referring to the simple ingredients and light and easy taste. Something better in quality than the larger, more well-known brands, but not too overpowering in terms of taste or pretentiousness.

The second "stream" they wanted to focus on was the opposite end of the spectrum. Mother's Brewing would also offer highly hopped, aged and sour beers. The kind of beers the true craft connoisseur appreciates.

This simple approach has worked well for Mother's. Their two types of beer offerings provide a pathway into craft beers and then a graduation to the fanatic level.

There is no better testament to how well Jeff's plan worked than a visit to Mother's brewery and tasting room. Their entry level beers appeal to the person who just wants a good beer to relax and enjoy. Perhaps someone getting off of work or taking out a date they found on *match.com* (hey, it's not just for finding brewmasters anymore).

The craft beer-ophiles find Mother's equally as inviting. Mother's offers a complete line of beers appealing to individuals who love unique beers, and they are constantly experimenting. Brian Allen may be testing ingredient pairings and looking for feedback, or he may be refining a new offering. The people who love craft brewing seem to love the fact they are part of the process of developing new offerings. It's almost a rite of passage for true Mother's fans to sample each step of product refinement when they are working on a new beer.

After some initial struggles in finding a yeast strand which worked in Springfield's hard water, business has been pretty smooth for Jeff and Brian. Additionally, Jeff has been amazed at the quality of people he has been able to hire and bring into the business. Like him, there are many people who share a love for craft brewing and are happy to be part of the company.

Jeff's idea of being part of the community has worked well, too. Mother's Brewing is an active supporter of local community events, often donating beer to multiple charities in any given weekend. In addition to helping out for great causes, these events have fostered a great deal of good will towards Mother's and has introduced the company to many new consumers.

For the long term, Jeff sees further expansion in Missouri, Arkansas, Oklahoma and Kansas. He wants to keep production levels and distribution limited to what he can manage himself to ensure they continue to offer the quality product their consumer base has already come to expect.

Based on the success they have already experienced, it's easy to surmise that the partnership of the brewing expertise of Brian Allen, the marketing/branding genius of Jeremy Wicker and the business acumen of Jeff Schrag is a match (.com) made in heaven!

Mother's Brewing Company Photo Album

Jeff Schrag

Mother's Brewing Company – Springfield, MO

A fun day at the office

Welcome to Octoberfest

The team at Mother's Brewing Company

One of the benefits of owning a brewery

Mother's Brewing Company party trailer

Mother's Brewing Company product lineup

Chapter 20
Odell Brewing Company

800 E. Lincoln Avenue
Fort Collins, CO 80524
(970) 498-9070

odellbrewing.com
cheers@odellbrewing.com

Established
1989

Leadership
Doug Odell, Owner & Co-Founder
Corkie Odell, Owner & Co-Founder
Wynne Odell, Owner & Co-Founder

"There are a limited number of breweries which could truly offer their products on a national basis. We prefer to stay within ourselves."
-Doug Odell

Doug Odell's first experience in home brewing wasn't great… and technically it might not even have been legal. When Prohibition was repealed in 1933, there was a stipulation in the amendment which made making wine at home legal but beer was mistakenly left out. Though not typically enforced, it's official status as being illegal made the brewing of beer at home more of an underground hobby amongst enthusiasts and not something which was typically done with a lot of fanfare.

This would stay that way until President Jimmy Carter signed new legislation making homebrewing legal as of February 1, 1979. Los Angeles resident Doug Odell's first experience in homebrewing came in 1975. Using the primitive ingredients at the time (only dry yeast was available, for instance), Doug made a very forgettable first batch.

Even so, he was hooked.

When Doug moved to San Francisco for graduate school, the placement office had an ad for a local brewery seeking entry level employees. His own experience in making beer piqued his interest in the opportunity. Knowing the beer industry, Doug knew exactly which company was offering the job. After all, there was only one brewery left in San Francisco. Doug applied for the job and secured a position at Anchor Brewing.

Saying the work wasn't glorious is an understatement. Doug was responsible for cleaning out the mash after it was used. His work in cleaning the brew kettle meant he literally had to climb inside of it.

When Doug decided to transfer schools, it meant he had to quit his job at Anchor. He hated leaving the company, but he hadn't actually planned to make a career out of the job.

One thing he noticed, whenever he told people about his job at Anchor, they were always fascinated by it. They wanted to hear stories about working for a brewery. The interest was always so strong he made a mental note that perhaps one day if he was ever looking to start a business, a brewery might be an interesting opportunity to pursue.

After graduation, he moved to Seattle and got involved in the strong homebrewing scene in the area. There, he also met Wynne, his future wife. One of the activities the two of them enjoyed doing while they were dating was to go to the local ale houses/craft breweries which were popping up all over.

After getting married, Doug was working in landscaping, and Wynne was working in finance. Rather than working for someone else, they thought it might be a better idea to work together on a business. Their choices were down to two: a landscape company or a brewery.

Is that really a choice?

Yes, Wynne and Doug chose what everyone else would have in the exact same situation, the brewery. The year was 1988, and Doug and Wynne felt that the proliferation of all of the brewpubs in the area meant the market was already saturated. They didn't believe it was a wise idea to stay in Seattle, so they began looking at other markets.

They ended up landing in Fort Collins, Colorado. Everything seemed to work there. The area was beautiful, the cost of living was comparable or lower, and the local beer scene was untapped.

The financing for their new endeavor would come primarily from Doug and Wynne who were selling their home and rolling their profits from the sale into the business along with Doug's sister Corkie who was joining them. They gave equity stakes to Wynne's sister and also a couple whom they had been friends with in Seattle. Those initial investors, along with loans from Doug and Wynne's parents, gave them the capital they needed to start the business.

With Fort Collins set as their home, they began working on their business plan. One of the first tasks was to establish the name. They did the due diligence going through the local flora, fauna and potential geographical names. Nothing sounded right until someone mentioned Odell sounded like a great name for a beer.

With the three primary shareholders all being Odells, it made perfect sense. Finally, the crew agreed on a name and from that point forward their company became known as the Odell Brewing Company.

In 1989, they found a location in downtown Fort Collins. They secured it and were officially were in business. They had a 15 barrel, 2 vessel system, along with 150 kegs to start. For the first six years of the company's existence, they were a keg only operation. Doug would literally brew in the morning and then head out to sell and distribute in the afternoon. Corkie managed the back office functions and had Doug's old job from Anchor (cleaning). Wynne used her finance background to keep everything straight with the books.

By keeping overhead down, they were able to maximize profits even in those early years. Soon they had not only paid back both sets of parents, they bought out their friends from Seattle and Wynne's sister.

That left just Doug, Wynne and Corkie as the only shareholders. With the exception of some stock gifts to senior management, it's an ownership structure they follow to this day. Doug notes it's a large part of their success. This ensures the only people having a vested interest in the company are the three which are there every day interacting with the employees and the customers.

Plus, they do not have the distractions of being forced to answer to outside investors. Having dozens, or more, is fairly common in the craft brewery world. Often these ownership structures lead to infighting and problems for the management. These are issues the Odell's team happily doesn't have to worry about.

The success of the company led them to moving to a new brewery in 1994. They expanded the business a few times along the way, but in 2009 they doubled the size of their facility.

Doug continues to brew the two beers he initially started with: 90 Shilling and Easy Street Wheat. In fact, 90 Shilling remains their most popular offering today and accounts for about 30% of their overall production. Doug laughs as he discusses how in 1989, 90 Shilling was so different than what was on store shelves there was some worry it may have been too dark of a beer and too overpowering in terms of flavor. Of course, when you compare it with today's beers, it seems relatively tame. It all comes down to taste, and the classic profile of 90 Shilling has proven to continue to appeal to buyers who have so many other choices.

The company is also very involved in the local community. Not only do they often open up their facility for charitable events, they also open up their offices for meetings for these charities. Often, Odell team members will get together on their time off to participate in charitable events like park clean-ups or building homes for Habitat for Humanity.

As they enter their 25th year, Doug, Wynne and Corkie Odell know exactly who they are. They have no visions of grandeur. Their only goal is to provide the best beer possible to their customers while remaining a regional provider in the Rocky Mountains and Great Plains areas.

Who would have thought a semi-good "illegal" homebrewer who started out in the business climbing into brew kettles could do all of this?

Odell Brewing Company Photo Album

Corkie, Wynne & Doug Odell

Odell Brewing Company

Filling barrels

Tasting

Doug showing off the solar panels

Giving back: building a house for Habit for Humanity

90 Shilling is Odell's most popular beer

Odell Brewing Company product lineup

Chapter 21
Red Brick Brewing

2323 Defoor Hills Rd NW
Atlanta, GA 30318
(404) 355-5558

redbrickbrewing.com
info@atlantabrewing.com

Established
1993

Leadership
Bob Budd, President and CEO

"I am a nuclear engineer by trade."
   -Bob Budd

Nuclear engineer?

It's true. Bob Budd was not only a trained nuclear engineer via his college education; he also made a living in the field working in business with controls and heavy equipment.

While that was how he paid the bills, food and cooking was always his passion. He cooked throughout his undergrad and graduate degrees and was an at-home chef after graduating. One thing Bob always noticed and didn't particularly like was the lack of use of some of the local products like Vidalia onions or Georgia peaches.

There seemed to be a tremendous opportunity to use the products from local farms and bring them to consumers via the traditional shopping experiences of the grocery store. When he noticed this void in the grocery industry, he filled the niche by starting his own gourmet food label. He packaged foods and condiments, both branded and private label.

He points to how far ahead of the game he was in the industry by noting when he started his company in Atlanta, there were only two other gourmet food lines in the market. By the time he sold his company 20 years later, there were 67 total competitors and a trade association which supported the burgeoning industry.

He planned to retire after selling his company, but it didn't take (it may be the only thing Bob ever failed at in business). His return to the workforce came about six weeks after his retirement. He was looking for investments with some of the capital he had received from the sale of his company. One of the investments he made was in the Atlanta Brewing

Company, which was the oldest craft brewery in the Southeast.

In 2005, the company ran into difficult times. Knowing Bob had a background in consumer goods via his gourmet food company, the Board of Directors asked him to help provide some direction. By 2006, he joined the company full-time and was officially back into the workforce as the President and CEO of the Atlanta Brewing Company.

Bob made several changes which in-turn got the company back on track. The first change was a shift in culture. He wanted to firmly build the company around the brewers. His goal was to empower them with the ability and desire to "own quality," to "own a sense of creativity" and to "own the sense of ethics" the company would need to thrive.

Bob also changed the company name. Red Brick Brewing actually came from a historic speech where the mayor of Atlanta noted the city will "rise like a phoenix from the ashes" and then stated, "one red brick at a time."

At a time when they were starting to sell outside of Atlanta, he thought it might be a good idea to take a look at the name of his company to avoid confusion or push back from consumers. The answer was a large scale rebranding instead a tweaking of what they already had in place.

He kept the Atlanta Brewing Company as the parent, but renamed the company Red Brick Brewing, which was the name of the company's beers. It may seem confusing, but Bob frames it out perfectly when he explains it noting the Boston Beer Company is the parent of Samuel Adams beer. People get so used to asking for the beer, it's easier to simply utilize a D.B.A. (doing business as) Red Brick Brewing since that's what most of their customers thought their name was anyway (very much like Boston Beer Company's customers asking for a Sam Adams beer).

In 2007, they opened a new facility which is very inviting for visitors on the tours they offer. Bob says the staff treats everyone just like you would welcoming visitors to your home. The team interacts with the individuals as they tour, which can number 500+ on a weekend day. One of the differences between Red Brick and most other breweries is the fact that everyone in the company brews. Truly, everyone the guests interact with on the tours has a knowledge of the brewing process, and how the company's beer is made.

Another winner for the company has been a partnership with the famous Vortex Restaurant in Atlanta. With its huge skull you walk through to enter the restaurant, it is well-known regionally and has even got a lot of nationwide exposure, being featured on various cooking and travel channel shows.

Red Brick Brewing and Vortex Restaurant have partnered on an Amber Ale called Laughing Skull. Red Brick formulated the beer and handles the distribution, and Vortex lent their famous skull logo to the brand. The beer is not only a great seller, but the dual branding increases the profile for both Red Brick and Vortex.

Even though he had never brewed a batch of beer before coming aboard the company he runs today, Bob's time in the grocery business served him well. With the benefit of hindsight, he knows now the daunting challenges he faced turning the company around. He believes it was a much larger task than actually starting from scratch. Luckily, he was well-suited to take on the job from his time owning his food company. He can tick off many traits between the two which are exactly the same.

For instance, both the beer and grocery industries are stagnant with not a lot of growth. Within that stagnation, though, the categories of craft brewing and gourmet foods were both growth categories.

Also, he sees the big guys in both industries trying to act small. They build huge brands through large distribution channels, advertising and large scale efforts to grow their brands. When smaller companies start to chip away at their market share, they introduce "smaller brands" under their name to sit on the shelf side-by-side versus their flagship brands. They are really just paying lip service with these ploys as they are cutting the same corners with their so-called small brands as they do their large and successful megabrands because the only thing these large organizations truly understand is volume.

Of course, Bob Budd understands quality better than most. Don't forget, he's a nuclear engineer. A 99.99999% success rate in that field means lives are lost. He follows the same protocol he did in the past to help ensure the success of Red Brick.

What does the future hold for the company? Well, Bob actually already knows what's going to happen. "How?" you might ask.

It's simple. Atlanta is always about five years behind what is going on in the craft brewing industry on the West Coast. Over the previous five years the industry has continued to grow and today accounts for approximately 18% of the overall beer business. Bob anticipates seeing his company continuing to grow at the levels he has witnessed over the last five years out West in his company for the upcoming five years.

Currently, their beer is sold in eight states. While he could envision them expanding a little further, he does see the company as a regional brand and will look more towards expanding within the markets they are in versus trying to expand further out.

Having two careers already, Bob does look ahead and sees a time when he will think about retiring. Ultimately, he plans to turn the company over to his employees through an Employee Stock Ownership Plan (ESOP). Nothing is eminent, though.

Bob's having way too much fun!

Red Brick Brewing Photo Album

Bob Budd

Where the magic happens

Exterior shot of the brewery

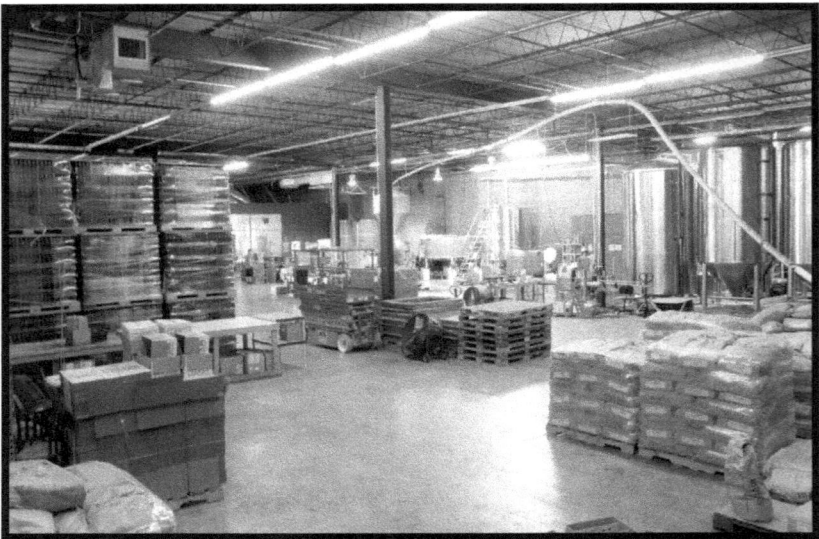

Interior shot of the brewery

The Tasting Room

Pouring a pint

Product label detail

Red Brick Brewing product lineup

Chapter 22
River Horse Brewing Company

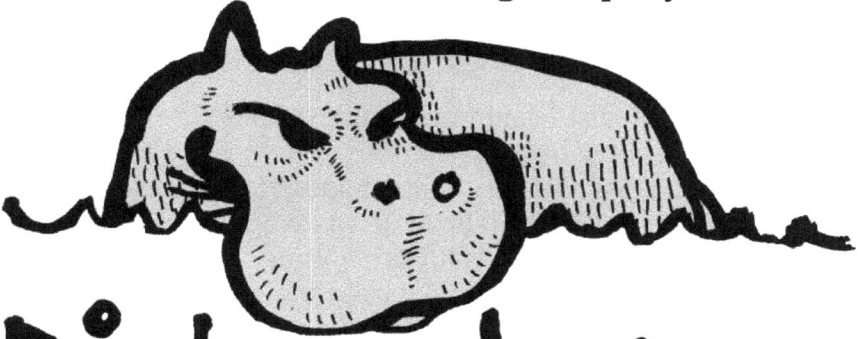

2 Graphics Drive
Ewing, NJ 08628
(609) 883-0890

riverhorse.com
info@riverhorse.com

Established
1995

Leadership
Chris Walsh, Owner & GM
Glenn Bernabeo, Owner

"We don't want to be one of those companies who put out a variety pack and one of the beers in the pack is one no one wants to drink."
        -Chris Walsh

If you had to guess the number of individuals from the investment banking business who had gotten out to join the craft beer industry, the safe bet would be zero. Seriously, it's not possible to make the leap from the world of crunching numbers to the ultra-competitive, slim margins, world of craft brewing, is it? Well, not only is it possible, it has happened. Two times over!

It's true. Chris Walsh and Glenn Bernabeo met each other in the world of high finance. Being about the same age, they had entered the world of investment banking at the same time. For years they worked side-by-side, first as associates in cubicles and then in offices as directors.

When they started their own business, their specialty in investment banking was helping distressed companies get their house in order to sell. These were often difficult situations. A typical scenario might be a third generation family owner bankrupting the business started by his or her grandparents.

For quite a while, they had a good business which flew under the radar of the much larger and better capitalized banks who really didn't want to assist businesses as small as the ones Chris and Glenn were working with. Eventually, they reached the degree of success where the bigger companies began to take note of their work.

Often, the best way to get rid of a competitor stealing business from you is to buy them out. That's exactly what happened with Chris and Glenn. In 2007, they got an offer they couldn't refuse, and they sold their business.

Far too young to simply sail off into the sunset, they began looking at new ideas to invest in. While their search led them to vetting 5 or 6 other businesses, when they found River Horse Brewing Company was for sale, it was appealing to them. It was a product they could relate to and understand (they were craft beer drinkers). They were close enough to the brewery where they could be there every day. They also knew it was an industry on the rise, and while River Horse had some issues, their business expertise could help turn around the situation.

While neither Chris nor Glenn had ever brewed a beer in their lives, they decided this was the perfect opportunity for them, and they purchased the company in 2007. Reflecting now on the purchase, they acknowledge what they ended up buying was the facility, a cool brand name and the location.

Oh, the location. What a coup it was to secure a craft brewery in Ewing, New Jersey. Think about it. The hot trend continues to be to buy and support local. They are on a line right between New York (the most populous city in the U.S.) and Philadelphia (the fifth largest city in the U.S. and a town known for its love of craft beer). The proximity of River Horse means it is considered a local beer for both of those cities and their 11,000,000+ residents. Don't forget the 8,500,000 other people in between, too!

Those positives aside, they did have their work cut out for them. The quality of the brand had slipped over the years. They lacked consistency in their beers, and it would be something Chris and Glenn needed to fix immediately. Doing so would mean a complete turnover of the staff and processes to brew their beer. They also redesigned their packaging and distribution model.

Every decision they made was from a consumer point of view. Not being from the beer industry, it was easy for Chris and Glenn to take the perspective of a consumer and how they would feel about changes since they truly were simply consumers themselves prior to making this purchase.

One of their first new hires was a brewmaster. The most logical hire would be to find someone who was experienced with another company and recruit them over. Initially, that was the plan for Chris and Glenn. As they interviewed potential candidates, they soured on the idea. It seemed each of the people they were talking to was trying to impress by telling them how they could assist River Horse by cutting corners. They indicated there would be minimal changes they could introduce which would only have a slight impact on quality but would save the company money.

Chris and Glenn weren't interested in shortcuts. Even though this was an established company, they were viewing it as a startup, and they believed taking shortcuts was not the way to turnaround the image and quality of their brand. They refocused their recruiting efforts on individuals who were just out of school. People who would take a "textbook approach" to their brewing and wouldn't cut corners.

After finding the right person, they actually shut the company down for 60 days. During that time, they were able to clean everything and let their new brewmaster get to work on reformulating their beers.

Chris and Glenn also went to work. They got in their cars and drove around to meet face-to-face with their accounts. They told the story of buying the brewery, shared their plan and took their lumps for the previous problems associated with River Horse. For the most part, these meetings were very successful with individuals willing to give them a second chance and a fresh start.

The problems of River Horse seem long behind them now. Chris manages the operation of the business and continues to be the face of the company getting out and making calls with the sales representatives from their distributors.

They have aggressive plans to grow their business from their current production of 13,000 barrels a year to 75,000 – 85,000 very soon. Improved legislation in their home state of New Jersey has really assisted in growing their business. The laws keep improving, allowing them to connect better with customers.

The most recent change allows them to serve pints onsite. They had been allowed to give tastings on the tours offered on the weekends but this recent change allows them to cap their tours with a glass of beer.

The "horse" in River Horse isn't actually from the equine family at all - it's a hippo. The original owner came up with the name since the facility is located right on the Delaware River, and the hippo had been used to represent sustenance and fertility in ancient Egyptian drawings.

One of the last components Chris and Glenn fixed with the company was the logo. They kept the name and concept of the hippo integrated into their branding, but they updated the look of the brand. Prior to their ownership of the company, River Horse employed an artist to design their label and logos.

The brand had a regal and beautiful look, utilizing the artist, but Chris and Glenn felt it didn't speak to the audience they were trying to appeal to. They hired a graphic artist out of Philadelphia who gave their product the fun and cool look you see today.

The enhancement of the branding has been another win for Chris and Glenn. Today, they have a 1,500 square foot company store in addition to an online gift shop where their merchandise moves quickly.

With the growth trajectory they are on, and positive vibe surroundings the turnaround of River Horse Brewing Company, it is apparent Chris and Glenn have taken all of the right steps to fix their company.

Who ever said a couple of finance guys couldn't become beer moguls?

River Horse Brewing Company Photo Album

Chris Walsh

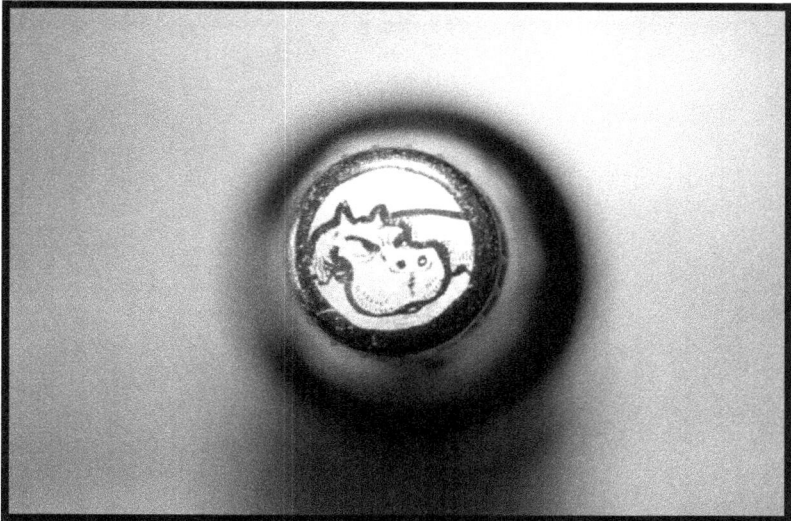

A River Horse bottle cap (you gotta love that logo)

Outside River Horse Brewing Co.

Inside River Horse Brewing Co.

Bottles ready

A bottle "really ready"

A look at packaging detail

Year Round Offerings:

Seasonal Offerings:

River Horse product lineup

Chapter 23
Rock Bridge Brewing Company

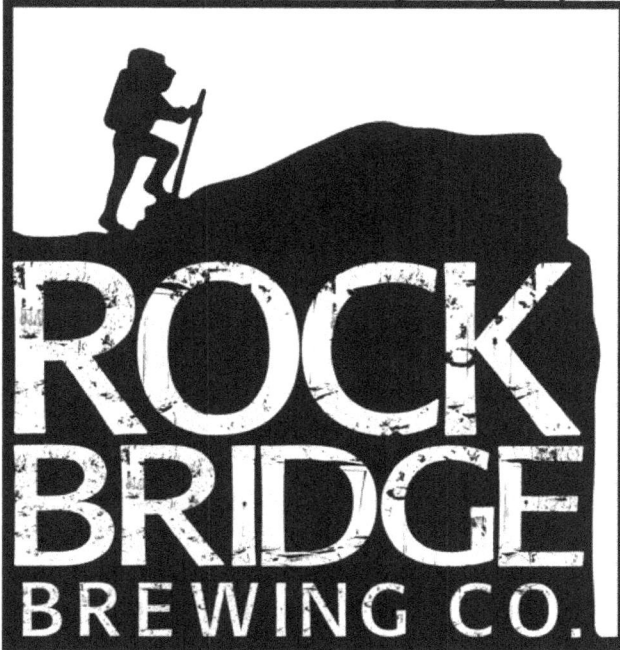

1330 E. Prathersville Road
Columbia, MO 65202
(573) 441-BEER (2337)

rockbridgebrewery.com
rockbridgebrewery@gmail.com

Established
2012

Leadership
Dave Brouder, President and Co-Owner
Stu Burkemper, Chief Beer Guy and Co-Owner

"The best part of owning a brewery? That's easy, we are making beer!"
    -Stu Burkemper

Quick quiz:
Without looking back on the previous page, where is Rock Bridge Brewing Company located?

It has an "outdoorsy/Colorado" feel, doesn't it?

Then again, maybe it's Utah. Don't forget they have those famous ancient rock formations and parks.

In reality, it could be anywhere, and that's the exact point. Rock Bridge owners Dave Brouder and Stu Burkemper didn't want to lock themselves into being a "Columbia, Missouri" brewery, which is, in fact, where they are located.

Sure, something tied to the University of Missouri would have been a natural. A tiger (the university's mascot), black and gold (school colors) or the iconic columns, which represent the University of Missouri, all would seemingly be appropriate themes for names/logos.

Dave and Stu were able to find the perfect compromise when they came up with the name Rock Bridge Brewing Company. Rock Bridge refers to a naturally occurring rock formation in Columbia, Missouri, which actually leads across a body of water: a true "rock bridge."

The bridge is the feature attraction at Columbia Rock Bridge Memorial State Park. The iconic wonder of nature is a popular spot and well known by the locals as well as the throngs of individuals who have attended the University.

Rock Bridge Brewing Company gives Dave and Stu the best of all worlds. Columbia, Missouri's past and present residents get a beer which to them is uniquely theirs. The rest of the world gets a beer which sounds oddly familiar, even if you can't exactly put your finger on where it's from.

Columbia, Missouri, isn't exactly the center of craft brewing in the United States. In fact, Rock Bridge Brewing Company was the first production brewery in the city. Bringing up the reputation of the City of Columbia is only one of the goals the team of Dave and Stu hopes to accomplish.

Rock Bridge (the brewery, not the natural formation) probably would never have come about if it wasn't for the mundane life of corporate jobs. Two individuals, whose bond was a fondness for brewing beer with a tie to Columbia, would have to each receive sentences to the dreaded corporate cubicles before they would have the motivation to get out and start their own brewery.

Stu Burkemper had attended the University of Missouri. He was a hobby brewer during college and enjoyed brewing so much, he worked one summer at a craft brewery in nearby St. Louis. After graduation, he attended Siebel Institute of Technology, the oldest brewing school in America, to hone his brewing skills. After completing the program at Siebel, he went back to the craft brewery in the Greater St. Louis area he had worked in the past. He ended up spending a year with them as a brewer.

As he started to settle down, he thought a corporate job might be sounder financially, so he took a position in government sales. It wasn't long before he realized life in a cubicle was not the way he wanted to spend the rest of his career, so he began looking for work, specifically in the beer industry. He realized if he could find the right opportunity, perhaps he could land the perfect situation where he could make a living and have some fun as well.

Back in Columbia, Dave Brouder was having an epiphany of his own. He, too, was relegated to life in a cubicle. He was in the insurance business as a claims adjuster. He would spend all day on the phone dealing with angry customers and angry management off the phone.

Dave had decided the best way to get out of the grind was to pursue his dream of owning a brewery. As his plans started to take shape, he advertised for a brewer.

Liking the idea of getting back to Columbia, Stu reached out to Dave. They hit it off and decided to go into the venture as partners, and Rock Bridge was officially started in 2012.

Initially, they offered draught beer only. They found it difficult to gain any traction. The bars which were open to selling craft beers tended to rotate their brewers in and out. As soon as they were successful getting a beer on tap, they would often just as quickly find themselves rotated out at another location.

Dave and Stu decided the way to grow their business would be through canning and packaging their beer. Of course, you need a great look once you go onto the store shelves next to the much larger and more well-known megabrands. Stu called on an old friend from high school, Curt Bean, to help him out.

Curt had been an U.S. Army sniper who served in Operation Iraqi Freedom. After getting out of the service, Curt had struggled with Post Traumatic Stress Disorder (PTSD). He had not only found solace in his artwork, he began offering art classes to veterans. He has found the classes to be not only therapeutic for the attendees but for himself, as well.

Curt Bean gave the company an identity and shelf presence which has assisted them in growing very quickly. In just the two short years they have been open, Rock Bridge Brewing Company has grown from a brewery selling in a small radius around Columbia to expanding throughout Missouri and adding distribution in Kansas, Iowa, Illinois and Tennessee, as well.

Their growth has come so quickly it has been hard for Dave and Stu to keep up. In fact, they have been so laser-focused on getting their beer on the shelves, they haven't been able to find the time to rework their facility to appeal more to visitors. This summer they finally have plans to expand to add a tap room to enhance the visiting experience (they currently do offer production tours but will look to increase interaction with the revitalized facility they now have plans for).

There are definitely no more cubicles for the future of Dave Brouder and Stu Burkemper. Their plans focus around expanding their business. They see an increased product line, more markets being added and increased market share where they already have a presence.

As unique as it sounds, Dave and Stu relish the idea of competition coming to Columbia, Missouri. While you typically think of competitors battling it out over market share, in this case, Dave and Stu see it differently. There is plenty of room to grow the craft beer market in the area. More competitors coming along can only help create an awareness and buzz about craft beer in Columbia. The way Dave and Stu see it, a higher profile of craft brewing will only help them in growing their business.

Let's not forget these are two guys who came up with a name intended to fall under the radar. Dave and Stu better be careful. If the rapid rise continues at the same pace, things may change for them. Their "subtle" tip of the cap to their hometown may change if they get so big everyone will immediately think of Rock Bridge as a Columbia, Missouri, brewery.

Of course, Dave and Stu are probably okay with that if it happens. In fact, at that point they may be so willing to promote Columbia, Missouri, as a craft brewing destination, we may see them come out with a Rock Bridge Brewing Company Black and Gold Tiger Columns Mid-Missouri Pale Ale!

Rock Bridge Brewing Company Photo Album

Dave Brouder and Stu Burkemper

Rock Bridge Brewing Company

Dave "hopping"

The fermenters

The canning line

Label detail

Cheers!

Rock Bridge Brewing Company product lineup

Chapter 24
Smuttynose Brewing Company

SMUTTYNOSE
BREWING COMPANY
105 Towle Farm Road
Hampton, NH 03801
(603) 436-4026

smuttynose.com

Established
1994

Leadership
Peter R. Egelston, President

"Initially our biggest task was convincing people we had a legitimate reason to exist."
        -Peter R. Egelston

Question:
You can spend your career teaching high school kids or you can work with beer. Brewing beer. Tasting beer. Experimenting with beer. Tasting more beer. What do you do?

Believe it or not, in 1986, that very question was posed to Peter Egelston. How did he answer it? Well, this chapter is about him, so it's pretty obvious he answered exactly how most of us would: he went for it!

In 1986, Peter was a high school teacher at a public school in New York City working on his graduate degree. While he wasn't necessarily thrilled with the work, he wasn't exactly searching for a job, either. One day, during the summer break, his sister Janet and her boyfriend were in town from San Francisco. The two of them (Peter's sister and her boyfriend) worked with a promotion company which sold merchandise at rock shows. They were responsible for setting up the merchandising outlets at the different venues of each stop of the tours for the bands they were working with.

While the job had been exciting at first, shuffling around almost every day for extended periods had grown tiresome. While they were visiting, they wanted to speak with Peter about a business idea they had.

Knowing Peter was an avid homebrewer, they came to talk to him about starting a brewpub. Over some of Peter's beers, Janet and her boyfriend told him about unique restaurants on the West Coast that were popping up where food was served and their own beer was brewed onsite.

Again, this was 1986, far before the proliferation of brewpubs we know today. The concept was relatively unknown, particularly in the Northeast where Peter was living.

As they continued to imbibe some of Peter's homebrews, the "chat" quickly evolved into a serious discussion. By the end of the night, the trio was moving forward with their plan to open a brewpub.

Starting from scratch, in an area where the concept was very unproven, meant there were a lot of challenges, the first of which was deciding on a location. They landed on Northampton, Massachusetts, where Peter and Janet's mother had grown up (they had visited there often as children to see their grandparents).

The timing of starting their business couldn't have been more perfect. By the time they had their plan ready to present to the bank for a loan, the economy was soaring. Peter jokes about the "vapor approval" process of the time. He states that when you brought in your paperwork, they would hold a mirror to your nose. If it fogged-up, you were approved.

Of course, he's overstating it, but they were really lucky in securing their loan just months before the stock market crash of 1987. Had their planning taken them beyond that date, they likely wouldn't have been able to get the loan which ultimately enabled them to start the Northampton Brewery.

Even though he only had been a hobbyist when it came to brewing, Peter was the brewmaster at Northampton when it opened. Scaling production up was only one of the problems. Securing the raw ingredients was another. Luckily, he was able to connect with others in the business. Even though there weren't a whole lot of individuals running these types of businesses at the time, he found those who were running brewpubs were always more than willing to share their knowledge and help out. They would network via rolodex (pre-internet) and not only share brewing tips, but sources for raw ingredients, as well.

There was a learning curve for the customers, too. Peter's favorite story from that time comes from an interaction between a customer and one of the waiters. The waiter was explaining the two craft beers they were offering at the time. We aren't talking anything really outrageous here, especially when you are comparing it to today's multitude of styles and tastes. Peter remembers it was like an amber lager and a golden lager. The customer looked confused and stated he simply wanted "an American beer." The waiter explained his two house-brews again. The customer once again reiterated he wanted "an American beer." The waiter retorted by pointing at the production area right behind the customer and said, "Sir, your beer is made 15 feet from where you are sitting. It doesn't get any more American than that!"

The customer's confusion was reflective of one of the greatest challenges they faced early on. People weren't used to the choices and beers which were different from what they were used to buying. Unfamiliar names and styles, which varied from the traditional German-style pilsners, meant individuals needed to take a leap of faith by trying these new offerings.

Through increased publicity of the burgeoning trend, along with other competitors entering the market, a demand did start to build for craft beers. By 1991, they were ready to add a second restaurant. They found a building near downtown Portsmouth, New Hampshire, and opened there.

Peter had been thinking about expanding the business by adding a production brewery (the breweries at their two brewpubs only had the capacity to produce enough to serve the customers of the restaurants). In 1994, equipment from a brewery which was going out of business was coming up for sale. On a whim, Peter quickly assembled a few other investors, and they were successful in buying the used brewing equipment.

Before the gavel even went down, Peter knew what the name of the new brewery would be: Smuttynose. The name comes from a small island off the shores of Maine and New Hampshire, just inside of the Maine line. It's a historic island which appeared on nautical charts going all the way back to the 1600s.

The year before, Peter had an internal contest to name the brewpub's newest beer offering. One of the employees, a woman who had vacationed on Smuttynose a lot as a child, had submitted Smuttynose. She didn't win the contest, but Peter loved the name. He felt it was "too big" to simply name a beer, but thought it would be best used for something grander down the road. Owning a brewery was something bigger. He ran it by his new partners, and they agreed Smuttynose was the perfect name for their new endeavor.

Within a month of starting their new production brewery, Peter knew it would be too challenging to have other partners involved in his business, so he bought them out.

With his outside investors gone, Peter was able to focus on establishing his production brewery while continuing to grow the brewpubs he and his sister owned. This was exactly the path they traveled down until the year 2000. Peter was looking to focus heavily on growing the distribution of Smuttynose, and Janet wanted to focus on the restaurant side. Knowing family ties are deeper than business partnerships, they felt it would be best for family harmony to split their businesses. The deal they worked out allowed

243 | P a g e

Janet to own Northampton Brewery, and Peter would own the Portsmouth Brewery and Smuttynose Brewing Company.

Today, brother and sister are both doing great in their respective businesses. Janet still operates Northampton Brewery, and it is the oldest continually owned brewpub in New England. Peter's Portsmouth brewpub is doing great, as well.

Smuttynose has an ever-expanding client base as it's now available in twenty-three states with two more in the works. Peter is quick to point out the company growth isn't just about casting an ever larger net. The company is very strategic about expanding their business in the markets they are in while they are concurrently seeking out new opportunities in different markets.

Recently, they have been working through the Brewer's Association and their exporter program. Being an active participant in the program means importers from other countries reach out to them based on their product and stated interest in exporting outside of the United States. They have already started selling in Scandinavia, England, Germany, South Korea and Puerto Rico.

The biggest news for Smuttynose is the recent opening of a new state-of-the-art brewery. They had been experiencing difficulties meeting demand for the last several years. The space of their new building affords them the luxury of having excess capacity, allowing the company to continue to grow for years to come.

Additionally, the old brewery was buried in an industrial area and not conducive to visitors stopping by (they really needed to go out of their way to find them). As such, they were only offering tours on the weekends. The new facility is built on an old farm and the feel of it still resonates throughout the building. This visitor-friendly set-up means they are now interacting with their customers seven days a week offering tours and tastings.

Peter also notes with the company's background in the restaurant business, they are a hospitality-focused organization. This plays out with a visit to their new brewery. The team at Smuttynose is warm and welcoming to all guests at their facility. They plan to enhance the experience further by adding a restaurant onsite later this year.

An interesting note is that the company has held onto their old brewery in the industrial park area of Hampton, New Hampshire. They no longer have it open to the public but are planning to continue to brew there. The goal is to offer a unique variety of small batch and experimental beers brewed at the old facility. It makes for an interesting dichotomy. At a time when the company is getting bigger through the expansion of the new brewery, they are also getting smaller by offering many more limited production and unique offerings through the old brewery.

One of Peter Egelston's early challenges was to simply convince consumers that his company had a reason to exist. He had to appeal to buyers who were skeptical there was the need for beer beyond what the heavily advertised megabrands were offering.

Mission accomplished.

Smuttynose Brewing Company Photo Album

Peter Egelston

Smuttynose Brewery

Smuttynose Schwag

Folks, that is a lot of beer!

Six pack/label detail

Smuttynose Brewing Company product lineup

Chapter 25
Spider Bite Beer Co.

920 Lincoln Avenue, Unit 5
Holbrook, NY 11741
(631) 942-3255

spiderbitebeer.com
info@spiderbitebrewing.com

Established
2011

Leadership
Larry Goldstein, Co-Founder
Anthony LiCausi Co-Founder

"Ouch! Look at this. I think I got bit by a spider."
   -Larry Goldstein

Larry Goldstein is chill.

In fact, he could be used as a living example of someone trying to explain the pop culture definition of chill, meaning: "one who is easy going." Take, for example, Larry's first foray into brewing his own beer.

He was a New Yorker in college studying biology in Atlanta at the time. As a hobby, he enjoyed trying different beers beyond the world of megabrands which dominated the shelves. Back then, there wasn't the beer bonanza you might find on the shelves today. His choices were limited to beers like Samuel Adams or Pete's Wicked Ale. Still, these were a notch above in both taste and quality compared to the heavily advertised bigger brands.

When he found it was legal to brew your own beer, he wanted to try his hand crafting some suds. He went to a shop which carried home brewing supplies. This wasn't the huge shops we have today with rows of ingredients and equipment, mind you. A relatively new hobby, you were limited to buying prepackaged kits with everything needed to brew already measured out.

When Larry, who wanted to go beyond just crafting what everyone else was doing, inquired about brewing a stronger beer, the clerk suggested buying the regular kit and just adding, "two cans of malt extract" to get the desired results.

Larry bought his equipment and ingredients and gave it a try. Something went horribly wrong and somewhere during the process and he got a layer of mold across his fermenting ingredients.

Mold?

No problem. Just vacuum that right up and problem resolved. Larry siphoned the mold off and finished brewing and ultimately drank and enjoyed his beer.

Chill move.

Ultimately, Larry would meet Sharon, a fellow New Yorker and future wife, who would join him in Atlanta where he would finish his undergraduate degree. After graduation, Larry attended chiropractic school. He and Sharon settled in Atlanta, and he started a chiropractic business.

The whole time Larry was doing all of this (undergrad, dating, marriage, graduate school, starting his practice and a family), he was brewing. He was also learning more about beer.

He found neighboring states to be more lax in their laws regarding beer, allowing more brands to be available. Soon he was traveling to try new beers. He also became involved in the beer community. He would trade beers or purchase online whenever possible. He jokes that his kids actually thought FedEx was a beer delivery company because they were at his house almost every day, always dropping off his latest beer purchases or trades.

He also actively kept notes on all of the beers he tried. His journal contained entries for over 5,000 beers where he would rate the selections and describe the taste profiles.

He used all of this knowledge to refine his own homebrewing skills. Soon, he was entering his beers in contests, and he quickly began to pile up recognition for his efforts.

It's safe to say he was consumed with beer. All of his free time was spent brewing. At work he would talk beer with his patients, often getting the benefit of them bringing him new beers to try. Gatherings of friends and family would be defined by Larry serving his latest offering. (He notes having friends provide you feedback is always an iffy proposition since they are usually pretty stoked to get free beer and tend to be pretty positive.)

He even got a part time gig at a local brewpub where he was able to experience commercial brewing versus what he had been doing at home. He spoke of opening his own brewery so much it seemed like it was inevitable his retirement from his chiropractic practice would be dedicated to launching his own brewery.

Well, that's how it seemed.

The future became "the now" one day when his wife Sharon, hearing Larry talking about beer for the umpteenth time, stated, "Go for it. Let's do this. Let's move back home to New York and have you start your brewery."

The next five years were spent divesting his business, selling their existing home in Atlanta and buying a new one in New York, getting a new job and working while evenings and weekends were spent launching his new craft brewing business.

Wait a second.

That is how you, I and almost every other person would handle this situation. We're not talking us here, though. We're talking about the Chillmaster.

Larry don't play that way.

Yes, he sold his business and house in Atlanta. Yes, he relocated his family to New York. He decided not to get a job, though, and just focus on starting his business.

That's right, Larry, a family man, with highly employable skills, was out of work to launch his dream of starting a craft brewery. Sure, he would do some part-time fill-in work handling chiropractic adjustments for vacationing fellow chiropractors, but for the most part, he was staying at home working on his new venture.

As Larry began working on his business, he struck up a friendship with a neighbor who had been a mutual acquaintance. Anthony LiCausi, normally worked days but while taking some time off work to recover from an injury, he began talking to Larry about his business. Soon, they were both contributing ideas for the business during daily meetings at "their office," which was Anthony's driveway.

One of the areas they were struggling with for this now joint venture was the name. One day Larry, on the way to the office (Anthony's driveway), cut through his yard between two trees. He ended up getting hung up in a spider web. Body twisting, arms flailing, he fought this seemingly invisible nemesis. As he finally "pulled into the office," Anthony asked him what was going on. Larry told him about the spider web, and as he looked down at his arm, he noticed a straight line of red bumps. A sure sign of spider bites.

As he showed Anthony his spider bites, the idea for the name of the brewery instantly came to them. They tried other ideas, but from that point forward, they kept circling back to Spider Bite Beer Co.

With a business plan in place, and a name now set, the two were ready to move forward with their business. One luxury they did have was time. Rather than going the conventional route of hiring a lawyer, the two managed to take care of everything on their own. When they didn't know how to handle a portion of setting up their business, they turned to their satellite office, the local public library, to get a book on setting up their company.

Sure, this delayed the speed of getting going, but all was still right in Chilltown.

It ended up taking about a year to get off of the ground and ready to start brewing their beer when Larry was called into action to assist his father when he became ill. For three years Larry assisted with the care of his father. In 2011, he and Anthony were finally able to begin brewing.

Initially, the two of them handled the distribution of their product, calling on and delivering their beer. Eventually, they grew to the point where they hired a distributor to assist in delivering the beer and getting it on the shelves.

Another duty Larry and Anthony handled was branding. A graphic artist had designed their logo. Since it was electronic, they could deconstruct it as needed and rearrange/incorporate other elements for their other beers.

When Larry crafted a Russian Imperial Stout they called, "Boris the Spider," they realized they had something special. Not wanting to simply rearrange their logo, they wanted this new beer to really stand out. The logo design ended up coming together on a Starbucks visit.

Larry noticed an employee on break sketching Wonder Woman on a pad of paper. This guy really had some artistic skills. Larry asked him if he would be interested in designing a label for Boris the Spider, Spider Bites' newest offering. The guy was glad to do it and quickly drew out and painted what would become the logo/label for this brew.

Spider Bites' Pale Ale is the company's most popular beer in terms of cases sold. Boris the Spider is the company's most coveted beer for the true craft beer fan, though. It has won more awards, received more press and is recognized by the company's peers as its signature beer.

While still a very young company, Spider Bite Beer Co. is growing quickly. Currently, their beer is distributed in Brooklyn, Long Island, Queens, Manhattan and West Chester, New York. They have just added another distributor and will soon be available in Buffalo and Rochester.

The company is also starting the next generation of its evolution with the opening of a tasting room and onsite brewing facility where they will be able to offer all of their products, plus limited edition and experimental beers.

Continued growth beyond New York will involve a lot of hurdles and obstacles. Rest assured, Larry Goldstein isn't worried about any of them, though. In fact, he's cool as a cucumber about the whole thing.

Would you expect anything else from the Chillinator?

Spider Bite Beer Co. Photo Album

Anthony LiCausi and Larry Goldstein

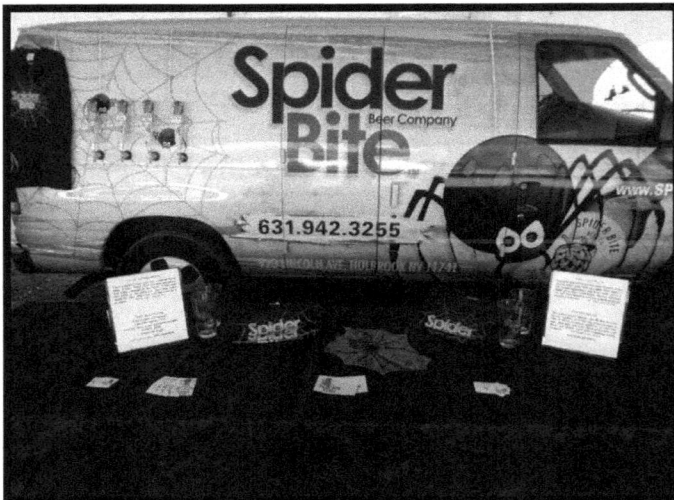

The Spider Bite Beer Co. event van (notice the four taps)

The beer connoisseurs' favorite: Boris the Spider

Boris the Spider logo detail (originally sketched by a Starbucks employee)

Customers connect with the Spider Bite name and it is very conducive to merchandise sales

Spider Bite Beer Co. product lineup

Chapter 26
Yards Brewing Company

901 N. Delaware Avenue
Philadelphia, PA 19123
(215) 634-2600

yardsbrewing.com
info@yardsbrewing.com

Established
1994

Leadership
Tom Kehoe, Founder and President

"I first began brewing in my college dorm room."
    -Tom Kehoe

Tom Kehoe will tell you the first real job he had was starting his own brewery. It's actually not uncommon for that particular response to come up when you are interviewing owners of craft breweries. After all, owning a brewery is often a lifelong goal for the enterprising individuals who start breweries. Previous work experience tends to pale to the magnitude of the endeavor of owning a brewery so they tend to downplay previous work experience. Typically, when you probe a little further with a few more questions, a richer work experience than originally offered up starts to emerge.

Not with Tom Kehoe.

He's telling the 100% absolute truth when he tells you he really didn't have any sort of career prior to opening up Yards Brewing Company. It all started while he was in college. He started crafting brews in his dorm room and caught the bug to enter the industry.

In order to learn the business side of opening a craft brewery, he and a friend went to work for a brewery in Maryland after graduation. Even though this would be the closest thing Tom would have to a job after college, it was really almost like an internship. He and his buddy weren't paid much, but they really didn't care. They were there to learn a trade.

They ended up spending two months there picking up the knowledge they needed to start their own company. In addition to the valuable experience they gained, they also acquired a fondness for English Ales since it was a specialty of the brewery where were working. Ultimately, this would carry over into their startup brewery and continues to be a focus for Yards Brewing Company some twenty years later.

Over the next four years, Tom would work a variety of odd jobs to make ends meet and put away extra cash towards his dream of opening up a brewery. He worked construction off-and-on when work was available. He did some acting, appearing in some local TV commercials. He even did the ultimate "odd job vocation" for a while: he was a carny. That's right, Tom traveled around with an uncle putting up amusement park rides.

Imagine if LinkedIn would have been around in the early '90s: Tom Kehoe, Intern/Construction Worker/Actor/Carny seeking next opportunity.

It worked, though.

Tom hoarded cash while working these jobs as he and his friend worked on their business plan for their forthcoming venture. The name kind of evolved on its own over time. In order to showcase their desire to feature English Ales, they wanted something that had an English sound to it.

The felt the word Yard seemed to have a place in the name. It was simple, short and had a natural English connection with Scotland Yard. At first, there were plans to perhaps incorporate it into a work sounding name. Perhaps something tied to railyard or shipyard, but they never got around to working it any further. Since friends, family, and yes, maybe even fellow carnies were asking when Yards was going to open, the name just kept sounding better and better by itself. By the time they were ready to open the brewery, Yards stood on its own merit, and the company officially became Yards Brewing Company.

The size of their operation was tied to the working capital they had. Not having a lot of money dictated the need to start small. Their first location was a three barrel brewery.

There, they were brewing only kegs, and they would sell and distribute everything on their own. At first, they were only brewing about 36 half-kegs per week. The good news was their product was well received and word of mouth was positive for Yards. They had no problem selling everything they produced.

After two years, they sized-up by moving to a new location. There, they not only had increased capacity up to approximately 3,000 barrels of beer a year, they also had the ability to begin bottling their product.

They stayed at that location for five years and then moved to a much larger location where they could once again increase their capacity. At their third facility they increased production up to 7,500 barrels a year.

In 2008, Tom bought out his partner and made a final move to their new state-of-the-art facility they continue to reside in today. Yards' new home offered several advantages over the company's previous three homes. The first being the location. Being on Delaware Avenue in the Northern Liberties section of the city puts them right in the heart of Philadelphia. Their previous locations had either been in neighborhoods or industrial areas and simply were not conducive to customer visits. This aesthetically pleasing brewery has a spacious tap room which is open every day, and they offer free tours on weekends.

The company also has plenty of room to grow. In 2013, they produced 32,000 barrels of beer and are on tap for over 40,000 in 2014.

The year 2008 was also big for the company in terms of its identity. Their product labeling had been based on a classic label from an old Philadelphia brewery. They had reworked it for each of their beers but all of their products had such a unique look on its labeling and packaging, it was difficult to identify them as being from the same brewery. Tom decided they needed some help, so they outsourced their packaging to a graphics company in Philadelphia. The labeling and packaging was given a unique look for each of their beers, but they incorporated underlying themes and looks which tied all of their packaging together. Now, you can tell from across the room which of the beers you see on a shelf are from Yards Brewing Company.

Though it is no longer a two-man operation, Tom has continued with the same philosophy for the company he always had: he's always selling. Whether it's making joint sales calls with his distributors, calling directly on stores or just doing some P.R. for the company, Tom continues to help promote the brand he has built up from a dream in a college dorm room.

Of course, going from 36 halves a week to 40,000 barrels a year means you needed some help along the way, and Tom is quick to point out the great team he has in place helping him. He notes that one of the greatest aspects of owning your own brewery is simply the fun. While you can have fun in any job, beer lends itself to a lighthearted atmosphere. Customers enjoy the product so they usually come in with a great attitude, and his workers are friendly people who enjoying interacting with the fans of their beer.

Tom sees continued growth for his brand and the craft beer industry in the future. Customers are embracing the idea of buying small and buying local so craft brewers will continue to thrive in the foreseeable future. The best part is that many of them represent new customers meaning they aren't simply stealing from the megabrands, they are helping grow the industry, as well.

It all makes you wonder how a young man, fresh out of college, was so confident in his ability to run a brewery he never tried to do anything else after graduating. It all comes down to the fact Tom had a fallback plan/insurance policy. He came from a family where almost everyone had been pipefitters. He felt he could always turn to the family trade if things didn't work out in the beer business.

It's safe to say the fans of Yards Brewing Company, along with his employees, are glad he never had to use that insurance policy!

Yards Brewing Company Photo Album

Tom Kehoe

Yards' brewery

Samples of Yards' cases

Brawler: bottle and case

Mmmmmmm

Yards Brewing Company product lineup

Did You Enjoy Small Brand America IV?

There is even more Small Brand America IV to enjoy. Each chapter is being sold separately through electronic book retailers with bonus material from author Steve Akley. Steve takes you behind the scenes of the interviews for the book and incorporates photos not seen in the printed edition.

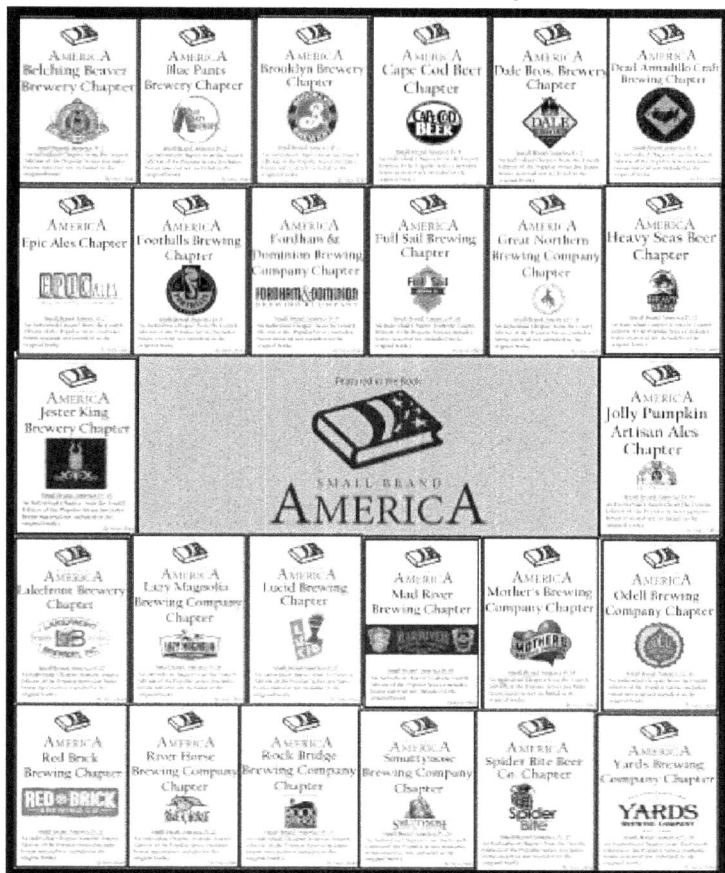

All 26 chapters are available individually through the Kindle Store, Amazon, Apple's iBooks and most other eBook retailers. At only 99 cents each, collect your favorites or the entire catalog!

The Importance of Online Reviews

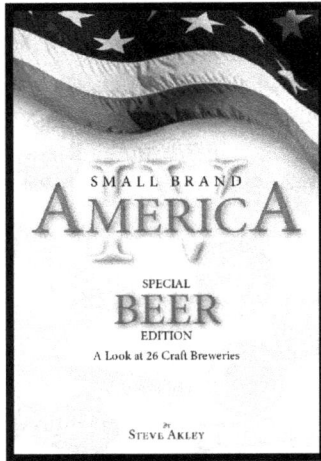

Reviews generate interest and create a buzz about the work of an author. Plus, your feedback is the only way an author knows if you enjoyed their work. Please take the time to review Small Brand America IV! Steve would love to know what you think!

Author's Notes/Resources

One of the greatest aspects about writing these books is meeting all of the great people behind the brands. Their personal stories, along with the stories of their businesses, continue to offer fascinating insight about owning a small brand in America today. Of course, writing about a subject as fun as beer doesn't hurt either!

I encourage you to learn more about these individuals and their businesses. To make your job a little easier, here's a recap of the websites for each:

Belching Brewing Company – *belchingbeaver.com*

Blue Pants Brewery – *bluepantsbrew.com*

Brooklyn Brewery – *brooklynbrewery.com*

Cape Cod Beer – *capecodbeer.com*

Dale Bros. Brewery – *dalebrosbrewery.com*

Dead Armadillo Craft Brewing – *dabrewery.com*

Epic Ales – *epicales.com*

Foothills Brewing – *foothillsbrewing.com*

Fordham & Dominion – *fordhamanddominion.com*

Full Sail Brewing – *fullsailbrewing.com*

Great Northern Brewing Company – *greatnorthernbrewing.com*

Heavy Seas Beer – *hsbeer.com*

Jester King Brewery – *jesterkingbrewery.com*

Jolly Pumpkin Artisan Ales – *jollypumpkin.com*

Lakefront Brewery – *lakefrontbrewery.com*

Lazy Magnolia Brewing Company – *lazymagnolia.com*

Lucid Brewing – *lucidbrewing.com*

Mad River Brewing Company – *madriverbrewing.com*

Mother's Brewing Company – *mothersbrewing.com*

Odell Brewing Company – *odellbrewing.com*

Red Brick Brewing – *redbrickbrewing.com*

River Horse Brewing Company – *riverhorse.com*

Rock Bridge Brewing Company – *rockbridgebrewery.com*

Smuttynose Brewing Company – *smuttynosebrewing.com*

Spider Bite Beer Co. – *spiderbitebeer.com*

Yards Brewing Company – *yardsbrewing.com*

Bibliography/Sources

*In addition to the websites of the companies profiled (all listed in the **Author's Notes/Resources** section), the following resources were also utilized to create this book:*

Interview with Belching Beaver Brewery Owner & General Manager Tom Vogel: May 12, 2014.

Interview with Blue Pants Brewery Owner Michael Spratley: June 23, 2014.

Interview with Brooklyn Brewery Co-Founder and President Steve Hindy: May 30, 2014.

Interview with Cape Cod Beer Business Manager Beth Marcus: June 24, 2014.

Interview with Dale Bros. Brewery Co-Owner Andy Dale: May 15 & June 10, 2014.

Interview with Dead Armadillo Craft Brewing Co-Founders Mason Beercroft and Tony Peck: June 4, 2014.

Interview with Epic Ales Brewer and Co-Owner Cody Morris: May 14, 2014.

Interview with Foothills Brewing President and Brewmaster Jamie Bartholomaus and "Marketing Guy" Ray Goodrich: June 3, 2014.

Interview with Fordham & Dominion Director of Creative Thinking Lauren Bigelow: June 2, 2014.

Interview with Full Sail Brewing Founder and CEO Irene Firmat: May 16, 2014.

Interview with Great Northern Brewing Company Head Brewer Joe Barberis: May 28, 2014.

Interview with Heavy Seas Beer Founder Hugh Sisson: May 28, 2014

Interview with Jester King Brewery Co-Owner Ron Extract: May 27, 2014.

Interview with Jolly Pumpkin Artisan Ales Founder Ron Jeffries: April 28, 2014.

Interview with Lakefront Brewery Founder Jim Klisch: June 27, 2014.

Interview with Lakefront Brewery Sales Manager Kevin Pearson: June 25, 2014.

Interview with Lazy Magnolia Owner and General Manager Leslie Henderson: June 24, 2014.

Interview with Lucid Brewing Vice President Jon Messier: June 26, 2014.

Interview with Mad River Brewing Company Brew Master Dylan Schatz and CEO Charlie Jordan: June 18, 2014.

Interview with Mother's Brewing Company Founder Jeff Schrag: May 12, 2014.

Interview with Odell Brewing Company Owner & Co-Founder Doug Odell: June 17, 2014.

Interview with Red Brick Brewing President and CEO Bob Budd and Marketing Director Tyler Cates: June 9, 2014.

Interview with River Horse Brewing Company Owner and GM Chris Walsh: May 13, 2014.

Interview with Rock Bridge Brewing Company Owner Stu Burkemper: June 19, 2014.

Interview with Smuttynose Brewing Company President Peter R. Egelston: June 5, 2014.

Interview with Spider Bite Beer Co. Co-Founder Larry Goldstein: May 22, 2014.

Interview with Yards Brewing Company Founder and President Tom Kehoe: June 11, 2014.

Photographs
All photographs, in the sections of each business featured, have been utilized with permission from the respective companies with the following exceptions:

Smuttynose Brewing Company
Peter Egelston (Lussier Photography), Smuttynose Brewery (Mon Petit Studio), Smuttynose Schwag (Mon Petit Studio), Folks, That is a Lot of Beer (Lussier Photography), Smuttynose Product Lineup (Mon Petit Sudio)

Special Thanks

To my mom, Sandy Akley, for her help in editing this book.

Thanks to my wife Amy and to my daughter Cat for just being themselves.

Hats off to Mark Hansen (*mappersmark@gmail.com*) for the great cover design. He's the greatest graphic artist you will ever find!

The following individuals from the featured companies not only couldn't have been nicer, without their help this book would not have been possible:

Charles Acker, Blue Pants Brewery

Joe Barberis, Great Northern Brewing Company

Jamie Bartholomaus, Foothills Brewing

Mason Beercroft, Dead Armadillo Craft Brewing

Lauren Bigelow, Fordham & Dominion Brewing Company

Bob Budd, Red Brick Brewing

Stu Burkemper, Rock Bridge Brewing Company

Tyler Cates, Red Brick Brewing

Ellen Cousins, Lucid Brewing

Andy Dale, Dale Bros. Brewery

Peter R. Egelston, Smuttynose Brewing Company

Sandra Evans, Full Sail Brewing

Ron Extract, Jester King Brewery

Irene Firmat, Full Sail Brewing

Tristan Gilbert, Heavy Seas Beer

Larry Goldstein, Spider Bite Beer Co.

Ray Goodrich, Foothills Brewing

Leslie Henderson, Lazy Magnolia Brewing Company

Steve Hindy, Brooklyn Brewery

Ron Jeffries, Jolly Pumpkin Artisan Ales

Amanda Johnson-King, Odell Brewing Company

Charlie Jordan, Mad River Brewing Company

Tom Kehoe, Yards Brewing Company

Jim Klisch, Lakefront Brewery, Inc.

Jessica Lucey, Great Northern Brewing Company

Diane Magrath, Belching Beaver Brewery

Beth Marcus, Cape Cod Beer

John Messier, Lucid Brewing

Cody Morris, Epic Ales

Doug Odell, Odell Brewing Company

Kevin Pearson, Lakefront Brewery, Inc.

Tony Peck, Dead Armadillo Craft Brewing

Michelle Robinson, Lazy Magnolia Brewing Company

Tim Ryan, Mother's Brewing Company

Dylan Schatz, Mad River Brewing Company

Jeff Schrag, Mother's Brewing Company

Hugh Sisson, Heavy Seas Beer

Michael Spratley, Blue Pants Brewery

Joe Thompson, Brooklyn Brewery

Irene Tomoko Sugiura, Jolly Pumpkin Artisan Ales

Marc Truex, Belching Beaver Brewery

Gina Vasoli, Yards Brewing Company

Tom Vogel, Belching Beaver Brewery

Chris Walsh, River Horse Brewing Company

Lastly, lots of love for my father, Larry Akley. He's always with us in spirit.

In Loving Memory of Larry Akley
1942 – 2012

Dad's badge photo compliments of Kelly Brooks (thanks sis!)

Love A Cat Charity – Honolulu, Hawai'i

Steve Akley proudly supports the mission of Love A Cat Charity with a donation from the proceeds of the sale of all of his books.

Mission Statement

Love A Cat Charity's mission is to help end euthanasia of unwanted cats by caring for feral and abandoned felines, spaying or neutering them and, when appropriate, adopting them out. Love A Cat Charity emphasizes the use of Trap-Neuter-Return (TNR) technique to humanely control feral cat populations. Cats are humanely trapped, spayed or neutered and returned to their outdoor homes. TNR improves the cats' health and stabilizes the colony while allowing them to live out their lives outdoors. No new kittens are born and the cats no longer experience the stresses of mating and pregnancy.

Support of Love A Cat Charity in Honolulu, HI, helps cats like this sweet kitty

Love A Cat Charity
P.O. Box 11753
Honolulu, HI 96828
loveacatcharity.org

About the Author

Steve Akley is a lifelong St. Louis resident. Small Brand America IV is his sixteenth published book. Sign up for his newsletter, or check out his latest work, on his website: steveakley.com. Steve also maintains an author's page on Amazon.com. Just search his name on the site. He can be reached via email: info@steveakley.com.

Find Steve on Social Media

@steveakley WORDPRESS & Steve Akley

Also by Steve Akley

The *Small Brand America* Series

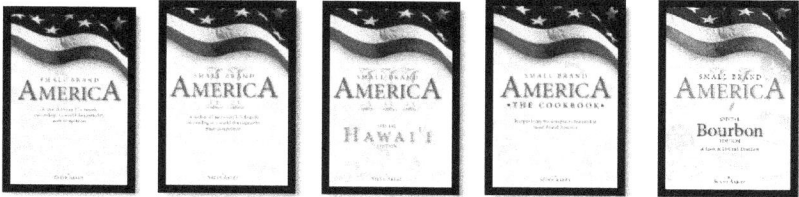

Other Books by Steve

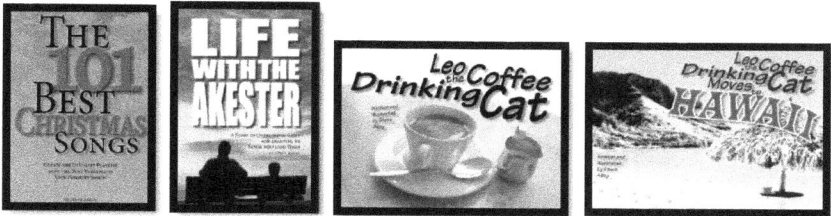

Steve Akley's Commuter Series

(Short stories available for Kindle, iBooks and other electronic retailers)

Only $1.49 each!

Be sure to check out Steve's website:

www.steveakley.com

www.ingramcontent.com/pod-product-compliance
Lightning Source LLC
Chambersburg PA
CBHW060543200326
41521CB00007B/469